Online journalism

Gabriele Hooffacker

Online journalism

Copywriting and conception
for the internet. A handbook
for training and practice

Gabriele Hooffacker
Leipzig, Germany

ISBN 978-3-658-35730-6   ISBN 978-3-658-35731-3   (eBook)
https://doi.org/10.1007/978-3-658-35731-3

This Palgrave Macmillan imprint is published by the registered company Springer Fachmedien Wiesbaden GmbH part of Springer Nature.
The registered company address is: Abraham-Lincoln-Str. 46, 65189 Wiesbaden, Germany

Preface

Online journalism and multi-modal, cross-media or trans-media work are omnipresent in editorial offices. In the process, it is easy to lose sight of the special feature of the online medium: the participatory opportunities to involve users at different levels of the online journalistic production process. They begin with blogging, where the boundaries between authors and users become fluid, and extend to the platforms of social networks with their possibilities of sharing and individualized information selection, to interactive moving images and playful applications in virtual worlds.

Forms and formats such as *scrollytelling, data journalism* or even automated text creation, so-called *robot journalism, have* been added. More and more standardized activities are being taken over by "Editor Al Gorithm". The fact that users are increasingly shifting to mobile online use requires not simply apps for the familiar forms and formats, but new concepts for online media.

In the process, online journalism has emerged as the focal point of current journalism education: It demands journalistic knowledge and skills in all media and technical understanding of everything hardware and software can do. Changes are happening in this area just as rapidly as in related topics of online law or social media applications. For this reason, reference is already made here to the website for the book http://www.onlinejournalismus.org for current supplements.

This completely revised 5th new edition puts mobile working in the foreground, especially in the conception. The two chapters on forms of presentation and participative forms and formats deal in detail with working on several channels, each in a media-specific, multi-modal way.

The description of the activities and requirements for online journalists have been adapted to current requirements. Without the classical journalistic craft it does

V

not work. The essential difference compared to traditional media is that in online journalism the activity of the users is included, i.e. interactivity is conceived and user communication is organised and moderated. The first edition of this handbook already described weblogs in detail, as well as participative forms and formats in general, which were still called "communicative forms" in earlier editions.

Anyone who wants to work in online journalism must have no fear of contact, neither with people nor with computers. We observe due diligence in our research, integrate audiences and cooperations, organize, write quickly and linguistically confidently, edit and process text, images, sound and film, get along with technology, think economically and understand how to work effectively under time pressure. In doing so, we are committed to the principles of the Press Code (see http://www.presserat.info), adept in personal conversation, on the phone and, of course, in online communication.

Anyone who feels addressed by this job profile will find the practical knowledge he or she needs for the profession in this handbook. For all those who are already active in online journalism, it provides suggestions for daily work and for training.

Much of what is inevitably described linearly in the book can only be made vivid online. For this reason, and because the medium continues to change rapidly, there is the site for the book. It emerged from the courses at the Journalism Academy in Munich as well as my courses at the HTWK Leipzig. Setting links or designing hypertext or communities can be demonstrated better online than in a printed textbook. Multi-media journalistic work only becomes clear online anyway; online supplements ensure topicality: http://www.onlinejournalismus.org.

Knowledge and skills related to hardware and software are indispensable for online journalists. Nevertheless, they are not covered in this book, nor is the necessary business knowledge. Both can be found in numerous reference books; the book contains information on literature and links. What this book is also not about is online research. All journalists need research, both online and offline, no matter what medium they work for, and online research is now a natural part of research textbooks such as "Research (Recherchieren)" by Markus Kaiser, published in 2015 in the series "Journalistische Praxis".

I would like to thank Martin Goldmann, Sebastian Gomon, Prof. Dr. Heinrich Hussmann, Prof. Markus Kaiser, Prof. Dr. Uwe Kulisch, Prof. Dr. Marc Liesching, Prof. Dr. Klaus Meier, Prof. Dr. Christoph Neuberger, Prof. Dr. Ulrich Nikolaus, Bernd Oswald, Peter Welchering, Sarah Just, Theresa Möckel, Kristina Mohr, Ruben Voss and other students and graduates of the HTWK Leipzig, to the participants of the online journalism courses for their ideas and the implementation of http://www.onlinejournalismus.org, especially to the courses OC-19 and PC-19, to

Bettina Pelzer for support in setting up the site for the fifth edition and to Peter Lokk for accompanying the book through all phases of the development process. Special thanks to Barbara Emig-Roller, Chief Media Editor at Springer VS, and Monika Mülhausen for project management!

Munich, Germany   Gabriele Hooffacker
January 2020

Contents

List of Figures

The Profession: Activities and Fields of Work

1

Abstract

What do online journalists do? To be able to conceptualise, write and edit a contribution for the internet or intranet, and to prepare and present the content audiovisually, requires knowledge of the journalistic craft – often not only of one medium. This chapter describes the activities and the necessary skills.

What online journalists do in online editorial offices, what they need to know and be able to do, is conveyed in this book. What scholars think of online journalism, how they discuss and classify it, is the task of journalism and communication studies. Where the fields complement each other, reference is made to them (Fig. 1.1).

This handbook of practical online journalism takes an empirical approach. This chapter first describes the *activities of* online journalists. From these observations, building blocks for the job description of online journalism are compiled. Where online journalists work, the article describes *fields of work*. In all of this, it becomes clear what online journalism is *not* and where the dividing lines run, for example, to online PR. Questions of recruitment for these diverse, sometimes very special tasks and the competencies within the editorial office are dealt with in the *organisation of staff and editorial staff*.

Insofar as the craft of online PR, i.e.: How do I get traffic to my website? is necessary for online editors, it is described in the chapter "The Online Users".

© Springer Fachmedien Wiesbaden GmbH, part of Springer Nature 2022
G. Hooffacker, *Online journalism*,
https://doi.org/10.1007/978-3-658-35731-3_1

Fig. 1.1 Gabriele Hooffacker, HTWK Leipzig, on online journalism and its special features (https://www.gelbe-reihe.de/online-journalismus/prof-dr-gabriele-hooffacker-online-journalismus/ or directly https://youtu.be/mOvHkK6jWWU)

1.1   Activities

The terms around the professional field are as diverse as they are dazzling: "online editor", "video reporter", "content manager" or even "social media editor" are just a few examples. I understand the term "online journalist" as a generic term for anyone who works as a journalist for an online medium, be it a web magazine, a community, a newsletter or whatever.

What do online journalists do? Being able to conceptualise, write and edit a contribution for the internet or intranet, to prepare and present the content acoustically and visually, requires knowledge of the journalistic craft – often not only of one medium: The cross-media newsrooms in the editorial offices are looking for online journalists who are trained in several media, who are textually confident, who are not afraid of a microphone, who can select image details, design infographics and edit video sequences.[1] This also means – knowledge of the appropri-

---

[1] To describe the journalistic craft for the individual media would go beyond the scope of this book. I refer to media-specific manuals such as Walther von La Roche/Axel Buchholz (eds.), Radio Journalism (Journalistic Practice), http://www.radio-journalismus.de, Gerhard Schult/ Axel Buchholz (eds.), Television Journalism (Journalistic Practice), http://www.fernseh-

ate user software, with the help of which the media-appropriate presentation is implemented. These are central tasks of the online journalist. What is not meant is the technical provision and maintenance of the web server or the setting up of the content management system, activities that are generally assigned to the network administrator or the webmaster. The focus of online journalism is on editorial, conceptual and content-related activities – this justifies the term "journalism".

An extended job description must also take into account organisational and commercial, i.e. management functions.

The daily routine of online journalism consists of sifting through mountains of agency news and selecting the ones that are relevant for one's own editorial team (news editor at the newsdesk), filming the award ceremony in the town hall or at a local company (video journalist), editing and streamlining an employee's contribution (online editor), hammering out the technical and financial details of the planned content partnership with cooperation partners (content manager), involving the co-discussant in the forum by e-mail and streamlining the online discussion (online moderator).

The fact that online journalism is not just about writing and creating, is typical of journalistic activity as a whole. Across all media, a division has emerged between the more creative *reporters/authors* and *editors*, for whom editing and management tasks predominate. In online journalism, there is on the one hand the job profile of the *web reporter* (finding, researching and implementing topics online), and on the other hand the *online editor,* whose work focuses on editing and processing.

The third group is the Media Producer with his company, a journalistic *IT service provider* that offers everything from a single source: *Conception of* text, image, audio, video, *organization* and *production.*

The tasks in online journalism can be grouped into three broad themes:

* Media-specific *journalistic activities* such as researching, editing, writing and publishing, implemented online,
* *Communication* with employees, customers, clients,
* Editorial *Management* Tasks.

Journalistic activities (first subject block) include:

* *Research* and *record* content from various sources.

journalismus.de and, of course, to the basic work La Roche's introduction to practical journalism, http://www.praktischer-journalismus.de

- *conceptualize:* write a multimedia script (storyboard).
- *present:* prepare and design cross-media and media-specifically.
- *edit:* Editing and cutting content.
- *Archive* and document content (content management).
- *Moderate* and organize communication between users and between users and editorial staff (communities).
- *organise* editorial information flow and communication processes (workflow).

Having good ideas (text idea, service idea, idea for online-appropriate implementation, headline idea, teaser idea...) is also part of it. This is where the area of *creative writing* begins.

Researching does not just mean, to be able to evaluate and classify online research and the selection and retrieval of information from various sources, whether via messenger, social media or as agency reports, but above all to enter into direct contact with people who provide information and opinions. The results are recorded: as a written note, in sound or image. The online journalist reproduces all research results *unaltered* – which does not mean that he or she is not allowed to edit, shorten and redact them.

Design a storyboard, a user journey requires not only good ideas, but also expert knowledge: of the topic you want to prepare journalistically on the one hand, of the media-specific craft on the other: How do I structure the topic? Which forms and formats do I use? How do I get excitement and variety onto the pages?

Presenting means, prepare the content in a media-appropriate way for the online medium and its various end devices: Deciding whether the interview should be published as audio, video or text, writing the text and distributing it to the different levels, choosing the image section and fitting the image, editing the audio file, selecting the decisive sequence from the video and inserting it at the appropriate point to deepen the text. The journalistic achievement lies in the selection.

This does not mean presenting one's own projects to cooperation partners or one's own team – that is part of the social and communication tasks of the online journalist.

Editing and cutting: What is finally presented on the screen has been edited by online editors: cut again, smoothed and shortened. Perhaps they write a new headline or rewrite the teaser and the opening page. Ideally, the authors have already delivered publishable content. As a rule, the final editorial work is necessary to preserve the image, the character of the respective online offer.

Archive and document: What the research has uncovered and what the editorial team has made of it can serve as the basis for further articles. With this in mind, one chooses when filing: What can be obtained anew at any time and can be deleted, what are valuable individual pieces that are worth keeping? Media archives need to be structured in order to make what you are looking for quickly findable. Freelance online journalists create their own private archives, editorial offices collect research results and finished articles centrally. The trick is to organise the editorial archive in such a way that the text, image, sound and video files can be retrieved sorted by keywords and topics. Technically, online editorial offices use editorial systems or *content management systems for* this purpose.

Facilitate communication: Communication, the exchange between users, is also content that the online journalist organises. The craft he needs is the moderation technique (cf. Chapter "Participative formats"); social skills and tact are also part of it. Experience is indispensable here; you can practice the typical online communication in social media and forums.

Organize workflow: From the idea to archiving, every piece of information has its *life cycle*. Usually several people are involved – this requires the exchange of information and targeted communication. Poor organization of the information and communication flow means at least friction loss, in the worst case loss of information. Project teams in online journalism often exchange information online and do not meet as often in person – here, particularly well-defined information and communication processes are necessary (see chapter Workflow and Content Management).

We have to master the typical online forms as well as the classic journalistic forms of presentation. This includes the conception of user/server *interaction* as well as *communication*. Online journalists have learned to separate information from opinion and make this transparent for their audience. Pure information is available to users in the form of *reports, news and reports*. We provide background information in *interviews, reports* or a more comprehensive *online dossier* that describes details and helps the user to classify the information. If we want to express our opinion, we call the contribution a *comment* or a *criticism*, sometimes we also write a *gloss*. We use animated graphics to inform (*flash movie*) as well as to comment (*online cartoon*). When we want to give tips and advice that answer the question "how to?", we write *service posts*. We also organize and moderate user communication.

For interaction as well as communication we use text, hypertext and audio and video elements, a mixture called *hypermedia*.

A special position is the online editorial work in press and public relations as well as in corporate media offers of companies and institutions (organisational communication): Here we work journalistically, but the goal is commissioned communication in the service of our employer.

A not unimportant side issue in online journalism is the technical media processing of the graphic, acoustic or cinematic interface: the more we understand about it, the better. But for us, such skills have more the rank of an auxiliary science: Especially at agencies, the technical implementation is the task of media designers. There is a clear distinction between the profession of online journalist and other professions such as web designer, screen designer, online producer and media designer. They design what online journalists design; we have to know the interfaces of the work areas. *Media computer scientists* provide the tools with which the online journalist works, *media managers* take care of commercial and organisational processes. In all these professions, online journalistic knowledge is an advantage in order to enable creative cooperation.

Do online journalists need to know how to program? It does not hurt. In many areas, however, the division of labour between journalistic work and IT is largely complete. In other areas, automated copywriting and data journalism techniques are becoming increasingly important. It is good when statistical and IT skills are added to journalistic skills.

Online journalists need to get to grips with their PCs and there in particular with the tools of the trade: the editorial system and if possible also the page description language HTML, the XML concept, the graphical HTML editor and the user programs for digital image, audio and video editing. We should be at least one step ahead of our users: in online research, texting and video editing.

Online journalism is a highly communicative profession. The organization of user communication online is one of the typical online journalistic tasks. It ranges from blogging and tweeting to email contact with users and the conception and moderation of communities. To do this, we keep our noses to the wind, travel a lot, both online and offline, and cultivate our contacts. We meet colleagues and exchange ideas with them, talk to the salesman at the chip shop, email the expert on nutrition, tweet and argue our way through discussion forums, follow the news in the media, are interested in trade fairs, fairs, festivals, in short: are curious about people and everything that occupies them. But that's not all: online journalists represent, advise and maintain contacts with cooperation partners.

Communicating runs through all the tasks of online journalists:

- during the research online, by telephone, personal conversation
- in the communication for user-site-connection
- in public communication on your own platform or social media platforms with users and colleagues
- in the cooperation with colleagues, clients, cooperation partners.

These tasks require people who have social skills and are resilient, loyal and fair – towards the employer or client, colleagues and customers.

Among the editorial management tasks, the third thematic block of the expanded definition of the tasks, can include:

- Market-oriented and brand-conscious design
- Think in terms of digital business processes
- Implementing concepts/organising their implementation
- Find cooperation partners
- communicate and advise in a customer-oriented manner
- Organize project work in frequently changing project teams.

Commercial activities of online journalists relate primarily to their own editorial department: *content sharing* means, for example, negotiating with the provider of the horoscope database, *content syndication* means taking care of the rights of use (licenses) for current music titles. If you take a look at the editorial office of any city magazine, trade journal or local radio station, you will find a similar mix of functions there: Customer contact at trade fairs or other events is often a task of the editorial office, the acquisition of cooperation partners for reader campaigns, communication with the audience and cooperation with authors anyway.

Building and maintaining your own brand – "Spiegel online" as well as "Süddeutsche online" are brand products – are also central tasks of the online journalists working there.

Acquisition of advertising customers and cooperation partners is not directly an online journalistic activity. In many online editorial departments, a separation between the advertising department on the one hand and the editorial department on the other has emerged. In other editorial departments, the activities are mixed – not always to the advantage of the online journalistic offering.

What must online journalists have learned? Employers value a solid basic journalistic education highly; technical knowledge and skills are also expected.

The German Association of Journalists has developed a proposal for an online traineeship (https://www.djv.de/fileadmin/user_upload/Infos_PDFs/Tarife_und_Honorare/Entwurf_Tarifvertrag_f%C3%BCr_Online-Volont%C3%A4re.pdf). Essential points: the "teaching of the basics of journalistic activity", the "teaching of the technical and content-related basics of the Internet, in particular computer/EDP", the "teaching of the profession-related basic knowledge, in particular self-image and ethics in journalism (press code)" and "entitlement to cross-media training".

An overview of training and development opportunities is provided in the final chapter of this book and the accompanying online supplement at http://www.onlinejournalismus.org.

Online media do not always mention in job advertisements and employment contracts their staff "online journalists", although their job description is clear. Reasons for this may lie in the lack of awareness of the job description, but also in considerations of the remuneration system: freelancers are occasionally paid fees that are below the minimum per-line fees for daily newspaper journalists. Permanent staff are sometimes given a fantasy title and a salary that can at best pass for volunteer pay. But salaries that are above the general pay scale are also paid – sheer impenetrable for those just starting out in their careers.

Employment relationship. Online journalists work as permanent employees or freelancers, as "permanent freelancers" with social insurance or as independent contractors. The "job description of a journalist" by the German Journalists' Association also includes online journalists: "Journalists are permanently employed or freelance for print media (newspapers, magazines, advertising journals or current publishing productions), radio stations (radio and television), digital media, insofar as they create offers and services oriented to journalistic demands, news agencies, press services, press and public relations work in business, administration and organizations, as well as in media-related educational work and consulting." (http://www.djv.de/fileadmin/user_upload/Der_DJV/DJV_Infobrosch%C3%BCren/DJV_Wissen_4_Berufsbild_Journalist_Torstr_JVBB.pdf, retrieved 27 December 2019).

Income. The range of earnings possibilities extends from a flat rate of €12 for an annotated link to impressive salaries and fees in the respective industry. If you work for a traditional medium, you can orientate yourself on the collective agreements for editors of daily newspapers or magazines, and in case of doubt also on salaries customary in the industry (e.g. in the IT or insurance industry). In media centres such as Munich, Cologne or Hamburg, salaries are sometimes higher than the standard rates.

The fee recommendations of the DJV and dju/verdi associations can serve as a guideline for freelancers, as well as surveys such as those published by Verdi's selbststaendigen.info (https://selbststaendigen.info/honorar-suche/).

To be able to do their job predominantly from home many people would like to be able to balance work and family life better. Those who expect this in online journalism right away may be disappointed: Of course, a lot of work takes place on PCs or mobile devices. There are virtual editorial teams that mainly coordinate online and only occasionally actually meet. But you cannot find topics or clients at home. Editorial work also often requires on-site presence. More often, you will find editorial teams organized around a mix of presence in the newsroom and a day or two in the home office. Even then, a large part of the work – and that means planning, project conception, maintaining contacts and presentation – will take place away from home. So flexibility is the order of the day.

Multi-talented people have the best chances: Anyone who not only does research on assignment but also develops contributions independently, not only has good ideas, but can also make the contacts themselves and turn them into viable projects, not only writes well, but can also implement his concepts, will feel at home in this profession.

This manual is limited to the central tasks in online journalism and describes them in the following chapters. The focus is on practical action: How do you write a teaser? How do you build a community? Editorial management, commercial, especially marketing knowledge can be studied or trained in, and there are excellent textbooks. Social competence is also acquired in practice, and can also be trained in special seminars and with the help of trained coaches. Online journalists should constantly update their technical knowledge themselves.

1.2 Fields of Work

Where do online journalists work? The fields of work can be divided into five areas:

1. The classical media with their online presences.
2. Pure online media: online newspapers, web magazines, portals.
3. Press and public relations online.
4. Mixed forms of advertising and journalism.
5. Intranet editors.

1. **The classical media with their online presences** have shaped the image of online journalism – similar to how the first radio journalists came from the press and later the first television journalists from radio. Bi- and trimedial offerings – press plus online, TV and radio plus online – are just as common as tri- or multimedia concepts. Cross-media editorial teams, which take care of the online presence of the parent medium, complement it and expand it in a multi-media way, are standard at publishing houses as well as at radio and TV stations. They design multimedia: the editor of the local newspaper decides which text will be published in advance as online news, whether the interview with the singer who

is coming to town on tour will be recorded as audio or video, or whether it will be written up as text in the print edition, or both. A TV feature includes not only the TV treatment, but also the development of the multimedia animations and at least one text contribution for the online pages about the show (Fig. 1.2).

2. Online newspapers and web magazines are **purely online media with cross-media content**. "funk", the public service for young people, is one of them, as is "Telepolis", a magazine about net politics, society and culture. In terms of structure, they are oriented towards online-specific formats such as blogs or communities and combine them with the action possibilities of social media platforms. Here you will find many elements such as voting, rating, sharing, participatory forms such as chats and forums, online diaries, additional services such as web mail or networking with other users.

3. Analogous to classic **press and public relations,** we call **online** press and public relations the forms of commissioned communication that municipalities, institutions, associations and companies organise in the online sector with the aim of communicating content to various target groups (interested parties, citizens, customers, members, journalists, etc.) and cultivating their own reputation (image) in the media and the public. In this context, online press relations (media relations) takes on a special position analogous to classic press relations: it

Fig. 1.2 Martin Wagner, Bavarian Radio (Bayerischer Rundfunk), on trimediality in public service media (https://www.gelbe-reihe.de/online-journalismus/martin-wagner/ or directly https://youtu.be/RVjGs69THjo)

communicates text, images, audio and video elements ("digital press kit") to journalists as the target group. The buzzword is *corporate media*.

Journalism purists and scholars alike have taken different positions on the question of whether or not corporate media is journalism. Those who ask about the activities in online editorial departments of local authorities or companies, especially in corporate media, the organisation's own media, can answer the question pragmatically with "yes". This is because, unlike in the advertising industry, the focus here is also on information, communicating opinions and providing a service to users. This textbook assumes that the journalistic craft in both areas is the same in terms of methods. At the same time, organisational communication follows a different set of objectives than journalistic work in an editorial department: strategic communication.

4. **Mixed forms of advertising and journalism,** characterized by the buzzword *content marketing,* are probably the most controversial border area of online journalism. Here there are online business models that are framed by an editorial offer, here you find media companies such as the online bookseller Amazon, for example, which simultaneously sells products and does public relations on its own behalf.

   Content marketing – the term describes this hybrid quite well. Is the content in the foreground or rather the marketing? The decision is not always simple and clear. What to do with the pharmacist information service of the pharmaceutical company with its medical news, the daily updated weblog with legal tips of the law firm or the reader service of the antiquarian bookshop with current book information? Such hybrid forms are included as a fourth possible field of work for online journalists.

   The best way to *distinguish* between the two is to look at the online products themselves: Communities like amazon.de or the popular travel and hotel review communities (sometimes with non-transparent user-generated content) can have an independent quality. If it is mainly about the promotion of products, recognisable by advertising language in teasers, texts and commercials, one cannot speak of online journalism – a virtual product catalogue falls under *advertising.*

5. **Intranet and extranet editorial offices** originated in administration and companies and are part of the public relations work of the respective organization towards its employees and cooperation partners. First of all, they serve the internal corporate communication and the *knowledge management* there. On a second level, information is made accessible to cooperation and sales partners via extranets. Sometimes, the third level is directly connected to the Internet presence of the respective institution or company.

Only some of the people working here are full-time journalists; however, they are often called "editors" within the company. They are mostly highly qualified professionals. Their main area of work is in consulting, service, sales; their job is to organise communication with their own employees, with partners or customers. Employee or member magazines, as well as business TV, can be seen as one kind of precursor to intranet and extranet editorships, the in-house mail and telephone system as another.

A threefold structure – Maja Malik and Armin Scholl take a closer look at those working in online journalism.[2] They make a distinction.

- a *core group of full-time Internet journalists* who earn more than half of their income from journalistic work and invest their entire activity in Internet offerings,
- an *inner fringe* as above, but who spend only part of their working time on Internet journalism, and
- an *outer fringe of* part-time Internet journalists who accordingly earn less than half of their income from journalistic activities and also work less than half of their working time, but at least ten percent, for Internet offerings.

The current Worlds of Journalism study for Germany follows the definition of the previous study,[3] if only to establish comparability. According to this study, the following also applies in principle: "Those who only sporadically contribute to media offerings or finance themselves predominantly from related areas of communication (such as PR or advertising) are just as little considered professional journalists as people who work as amateur or hobby journalists (e.g. as bloggers).[4] The Federal Employment Agency defines it quite differently in its statistics: According to this, more than 220,000 people exercise an occupation in editing and journalism, publishing and media business or in public relations, and the trend is

---

[2] Maja Malik, Armin Scholl, Eine besondere Spezies. Strukturen und Merkmale des Internet-Journalismus. In: Christoph Neuberger, Christian Nuernbergk, Melanie Rischke (Hrsg.): Journalismus im Internet: Profession – Partizipation – Technisierung (Wiesbaden: VS-Verlag 2009, S. 169–195, hier: S. 171 ff.).

[3] Siegfried Weischenberg (ed.): Die Souffleure der Mediengesellschaft. Report on Journalists in Germany (UVK, Konstanz 2006).

[4] Nina Steindl, Corinna Lauerer, Thomas Hanitzsch, Journalismus in Deutschland. Aktuelle Befunde zu Kontinuität und Wandel im deutschen Journalismus. (Publizistik 2017, 62: S. 401–423).

rising.[5] Of these, 158,000, or 72%, are counted as working in editorial and journalism.

How many online journalists are there now in the German-speaking world?

Since neither the employment agency nor the aforementioned studies differentiate according to media sectors, it is not so easy to say. The only thing that is certain is that the constantly increasing total number of journalists is due to the growing field of online journalism. In an evaluation of job offers, those for online journalists far outweighed those for traditional journalists. It can be assumed that the majority of the 158,000 journalists work partly or entirely in online journalistic fields of activity.[6]

Demarcation: Online editors who contribute texts for the Internet and intranet as part of their full-time work in companies or institutions cannot be included in the figures. Among them, too, the share of writing for online media is increasing. They are quite rightly listed with their main occupation in the statistics of the Employment Agency.

Volunteer publishers are also not to be counted among those professionally active in online journalism. The entire field of amateur or citizen journalism online cannot be valued highly enough in terms of the innovations it generates and its overall impact on society. When it comes to professional activity, i.e. paid activity, it cannot be taken into account.

For intranet editors there are numerous overlaps with online journalistic activities in terms of craftsmanship: from the procurement of information and its structuring (content management) to media-appropriate preparation. The technical basis (content management systems, participative and community elements, workflows determined by the editorial system) is also identical to that of a "pure" online editorial department. For this reason, intranet and extranet editorial teams have been included as a field of work; this handbook is explicitly aimed at them as well.

---

[5] Blickpunkt Arbeitsmarkt, April 2019: Akademikerinnen und Akademiker. https://statistik. arbeitsagentur.de/Statischer-Content/Arbeitsmarktberichte/Berufe/generische-Publikationen/Broschuere-Akademiker.pdf

[6] Gabriele Hooffacker, Peter Lokk, Online-Journalisten – wer, wie, was, und wenn ja, wie viele? In: Gabriele Hooffacker, Cornelia Wolf (Hg.), Technische Innovationen – Medieninnovationen? (Wiesbaden: Springer VS, 2016, S. 34–46).

1.3   Staff and Editorial Organization

We have described the job description of online journalists, including fields of work, tasks and earning potential. So many-sided trained online journalists – how and where do you find them? Journalism schools are the first choice when looking for staff, universities and colleges are now almost on an equal footing with them: Their training has become more practical than was the case twenty years ago. Many courses of study, training and further education include work placements: a good opportunity for both sides to get to know each other. The addresses of such training and further education institutions can be found in the chapter "Training and further education".

Which employment relationship a media company chooses, depends on all sorts of commercial considerations and not least the philosophy of the company. The editorial workflows need to be clarified: What work has to be organized by regularly present editors, what can be outsourced to external staff?

Editors and authors/reporters let the online product come into being. (For marketing and other tasks that are not primarily journalistic, please consult the relevant websites and specialist literature). Whether the editor-in-chief has to be more of a creative journalist or a top manager is a question that cannot be answered definitively – probably both.

Without permanent editors no sensible editorial work can be done. Every medium has had to make this experience, since journalism means that planning, organising and publishing takes place on a regular basis. How this permanent co-operation is organised in terms of labour law – in the form of a permanent position or as a contractually regulated freelance, self-responsible entrepreneurial activity – is left to the parties involved, especially the employer.

The permanent employee is integrated into the regular work processes; he has a fixed workplace in the editorial office. There is nothing to prevent him from doing some of his work from home – but he will spend the greater part of the week in the editorial office. His involvement in team tasks – planning the overall site, meetings between different departments, coordination of freelancers – is too great for this.

The freelancer, with their ideas, contacts and enjoyment of researching and writing, as well as smart technical solutions, are an important content supplier. They can be found through targeted searches in career portals such as LinkedIn or Xing, in journalist networks (good references are the be-all and end-all), through their own online advertisements (here the problem of the right selection criteria arises) and not least by studying competitor products.

Sometimes permanent employees become freelancers because their life situation has changed, the reverse is also possible. **The editorial organization is in a state of flux.** The classic editorial department with its division into sections, such as politics – local affairs – business – feature pages – sports, has been replaced across the board by an integrated newsroom in which editors work together on a topic-oriented basis. Klaus Meier described these shifts in his dissertation.[7] His conclusion: In extreme cases, the classic departments have been completely dissolved; project teams work together on a topic-oriented basis. Gradually, a differentiation of tasks can be observed again: Professional video teams support the online editors, external experts contribute their expertise.

Designate a responsible person. The little word "team" can be dissolved as: "Great: someone else does it". As nice as teamwork is: There must be one person who bears the final responsibility. The "editor on duty" or "chief of staff" ensures that the schedule and the overall concept are adhered to. One possibility: Everything that is published online must be approved by him. Too many control bodies, on the other hand, do not make the online publication any better – only less up-to-date.

For the intranet, such an instance is only conditionally necessary. Here, everyone should be allowed to publish and release within their competencies and their position in the hierarchy. Irrespective of this, it is recommended that texts are proofread by a colleague before they are published (dual control principle).

Team and project management. The work of online journalists consists, among other things, of planning, organising and designing content, developing suitable organisational structures, avoiding frictional losses, using optimal communication possibilities, working with existing structured data and developing cooperation concepts.

Own volunteers, trainees, guest students or interns can shape the company's own way of working. Whoever invests here, employs experienced staff to supervise and takes the training of young colleagues seriously, has the chance of being able to fall back on well-trained permanent or freelance staff in the longer term. Even if the well-trained volunteer then moves to another company: keeping in touch is worthwhile. Perhaps you will work together again later – with benefits for both sides.

IT knowledge is needed by online journalists more than press, radio or television journalists, because they not only have to use it for copywriting or production, but also in the publication process: They use the editorial system to enter files or

---

[7] Klaus Meier, Ressort, Sparte, Team. Wahrnehmungsstrukturen und Redaktionsorganisation im Zeitungsjournalismus (UVK, Konstanz 2002).

quickly hack a news item into the PC, which they publish immediately. In many online editorial departments, however, that is the end of the technical story: the basic design of the website was created by a team of graphic designers, the database was programmed by a specialist, and there are media designers who take care of the audio and video elements. The daily workflow is essentially determined by the editorial system (also: content management system, CMS for short).

Minimum technical requirements for online journalists

1. Solid basic knowledge of desktop PC and mobile device of any operating system,
2. Secure user knowledge of the editorial system and communication software used,
3. User knowledge in digital image processing as well as in audio and video editing programs,
4. intensive user knowledge of how the web works and common tools available online,
5. Knowledge of current surveys on user behavior and search engine optimization.

Security in dealing with files, folder structures, networks and multiple servers falls under the first point: On which server is internal data located (production server), on which is it published (publication or live server)? Online journalists have to cope with different file formats and their particularities. And of course they know that the Word document they have just written will not be published on the Internet – or they understand why the editorial system is necessary in the first place.

Quickly familiarized with the respective editorial system then secondly, who has solid PC skills, – provided there is proper training for the new employee. An online journalist who is obviously struggling with his software (with the program winning the battle) does not make a competent impression on users when they notice that the photo is missing or the links do not work. Appropriate user knowledge can be acquired quickly – and should be.

Which program should you learn? Here, the rule of thumb applies: Anyone who has mastered one representative of a software genre is usually able to familiarize himself with another product of the same genre through self-study. In concrete terms: Anyone who can use the image editing program Photoshop will quickly become familiar with the product Gimp; anyone who knows the video editing software Premiere will also find their way around Avid or DaVinci Resolve after a briefing.

Digital audio and video editing is (thirdly) only one side. In addition, there must be journalistic training that includes at least basic elements of radio and television journalism. However, the editorial departments of the broadcasting stations increasingly expect their employees to deliver ready-produced contributions – not only in online journalism.

Therefore, it is recommended that online journalists master at least one program for digital audio editing and one for video editing.

As users themselves know very well (fourth) online journalists need to know the medium of the Internet and the associated software products, such as common apps on smartphones, in order to be able to assess user behaviour and design competently for the medium. All this requires knowledge of user programs, i.e. ready-made software tools. In addition, they must know where the limits of the tools available to him lie. They should be able to roughly estimate how elaborate it is, for example, to design an animated graphic or to build an interactive statistic.

What users are looking for, online journalists need to know. Knowledge of the relevant surveys and studies is a prerequisite; they must be familiar with search engine optimization for text, audio and video contributions. Observing current trends is also one of their tasks.

Editorial systems allow the complete administration and updating of an intranet or web presence by a multi-headed editorial team. To avoid confusion when publishing, editorial systems work with access rights. Templates contain design specifications for the layout. With most editorial systems, they can be predefined. Similar to how a newspaper editor often writes directly into the layout program with his defined design framework, the online editor is already defined by the layout through the templates.

Authoring systems offer extensive multimedia design functions beyond the performance spectrum of editorial systems. Originally developed as a development tool for learning systems on CD-ROM, they are intended for the conception and design of complex web and intranet offerings. Current authoring systems manage all components from text and images to sound and film sequences.

Multimedia software tools are often additionally required when it comes to content management between two different media, for example the online presence of a daily newspaper or a radio station. In this case, the online journalist must be familiar enough with the technology of both media to be able, for example, to prepare the photos he receives in a data format suitable for the magazine for the Internet – or at least know that this is necessary.

Because the file formats are typical for the media. At the press/online interface, for example, the texts and images may flow into the layout on the one hand, but on the other hand they have to be converted for the Internet – by whatever means. There are similar peculiarities at the radio/online and television/online interfaces. Online videos do not have to be in HD format, and not every television format is suitable for playback on a mobile phone.

Databases play an essential role in online journalism. They form the basis of every good editorial system, as they are the prerequisite for systematic entry and archiving of contributions. A good content management system allows the tagging of articles (text, image, sound, video), supports full-text search and handles the preparation of dynamic content for the user.

Assign meaningful keywords, is not a question to be solved by software, but a core task of the editors. After all, keywording is essential for search engine optimization. From a librarian's point of view, a distinction is made between keyword (generic term) and headword (occurs in the text). Keywords belong to the meta information, keywords are important for full text search. Keywords are also responsible for finding and linking similar content. It is therefore all the more important that they are assigned according to uniform criteria.

Web design tools are software products that the media designer needs – the journalist not necessarily. What the online journalist needs to know depends on the respective workplace and can therefore not be answered in general terms. Those who want to know what is going on in the background of their editorial system cannot avoid the topics HTML, XML and XHTML. But also those who work with an editorial system or one of the web design tools should have understood how HTML works. In an emergency, you are then able to make a few changes by hand in the source code.

This manual is not a textbook for HTML or XML and certainly not a programming manual – I refer to relevant works, especially the website and the books by Stefan Münz.

Courses and seminars for your own employees qualify online journalists in journalistic craft, technical know-how and soft skills, as social skills are called in new German. The decision whether to offer specially tailored in-house training or to participate in external open seminars, whether in-house trainers or external ones, is often made jointly by the editorial manager and the HR department. One proven model is training budgets in the form of time and money allotted to each employee. – The fact that drastic organisational changes – the introduction of a new editorial system, changes in the editorial organisation – must be well prepared in training courses and seminars serves the purpose of quality assurance. An overview of seminar providers can be found in relevant trade journals and online offers as well as in the chapter "Training and further education".

Further Reading

1. Deutscher Journalist/innenverband (Hrsg): Berufsbild des Journalist/innen, https://www.
   djv.de/fileadmin/user_upload/Der_DJV/DJV_Infobrosch%C3%BCren/DJV_Wissen_4_
   Berufsbild_Journalist_Torstr_JVBB.pdf (jeweils aktuelle Ausgabe)
2. La Roches Einführung in den praktischen Journalismus. Mit genauer Beschreibung aller
   Ausbildungswege (Journalistische Praxis), jeweils aktuelle Auflage
3. Klaus Meier, Journalistik (UVK, Konstanz, jeweils letzte Ausgabe)

Further Link

4. https://onlinejournalismus.de

The Medium

2

Abstract

How do online media differ from the others? What is the relationship between online journalism and journalism in the press, radio and television? Active users can be reached with interactive concepts – this is the subject of the first article in this chapter. Definitions of online journalistic forms follow in the next article. The constant presence of technology is changing and shaping online editorial processes, the *workflow*. The possibilities of content *management* range from content sharing to intelligent database concepts and dynamic content.

2.1   What Is Online Journalism?

Writing for online media is first and foremost: more than writing. Visual thinking is a prerequisite, but so is acoustic and cinematic planning and design, and above all, the conceptualization of non-linear sequences. The playback media are: Screen and speaker – not dissimilar to television journalism. Text and image provide the basic information. The linking of text, image, video and audio elements goes beyond the classic matt screen.

Write for the users: The main difference between online media and all classic mass media, however, lies in the activity of the user: via touch screen or mouse, users have the power of command over the online medium; they navigate automatically through hypermedia. Above all, however, they communicate directly with other users – something that none of the other media could originally offer.

That is what makes producing for the web so exciting. Online journalists have to think of the users as part of their work. What do they want? Who or what are they

Fig. 2.1 Christoph Neuberger, Free University of Berlin, on journalism on the Internet and the identity crisis in journalism (https://www.gelbe-reihe.de/online-journalismus/prof-dr-christoph-neuberger/oder direct https://youtu.be/Ul9InZoXCxo)

looking for? How do they go about it? What is the best way to help them find what they need? (Fig. 2.1).

What is the goal of the users on the online site, that you design? Everyone wants to reach their goal quickly online – if only to save time and money. The tools of market research help to find out what this means specifically for special offers.

Studies on the behavior of users on the Internet are necessary tools for planning successful online offers. The chapter "Online users" provides an introduction.

Select active is what makes online services so appealing. First and foremost, alternatives must be visible: Every good online page leads to others. But if you have a choice, you are spoilt for choice: too many options confuse you. It also causes annoyance when a link does not reveal what the announcement suggests. Users want to know in advance what they are getting into. And they certainly do not want to have something forced on them against their will, but rather make a conscious decision.

Media Comparison

Print	Radio	Television	Online
Reader has full control over time	Listener is bound to the time schedule of the programme; delayed retrieval possible	Viewer is bound to the time schedule of the programme, delayed retrieval possible	User has full control over time
Can: browse, put away	Can: listen away, switch off, do something else on the side	Can: do something else on the side, zap	Can: select, click, enter something, surf away – side activities individually possible
Linear text, visual text elements and images provide reading stimuli and help with orientation and comprehension	Acoustic packaging elements, vocal signals and repetitions help you to quickly find your way around, even when you are listening in passing	Optical and acoustic signals, colours, repetitions, interplay of still/ moving image, spoken/inserted text convey information and the overall picture	Text, sound, image and film elements are partly faded in, for the most part the user has their sequence in hand. Text, optical and acoustic signals help with navigation
Journalist writes text, illustrates with photos and graphics	Journalist speaks and illustrates with sound elements	Journalist writes script, acts in front of and behind camera	Journalist writes a script for the user to "play himself"
Feedback by letter to the editor (phone call, fax, e-mail...), which will be *printed*	Listener telephone, "request programmes", competitions for listener loyalty	Calls, viewer mail, faxes and e-mails, guessing and sweepstakes, digital polls, reality TV	Communication between users, real-time chat with invited guests and other users, WebCams, live streams with user activity, time-delayed discussion forums, voting, users' own contributions (text, sound, image...), joint games and competitions ...

What users do not want, is above all: to be helpless without orientation in front of an unmanageable online offer. You do *not* want

- have to search for a long time
- be misled
- are overfed and distracted by too much information ("information overload")

- end-up in dead ends
- and by no means: lose the overview.

But that is not so easy. Because in contrast to the print medium, the user cannot scroll online, but must "scroll" or continue clicking or tapping. They quickly lose sight of the original page.

Crutches and aids there are many: Tables of contents, often fold-out, on the screen, visual and text signals ('You are now here: → News and Media → Journalism'). Site maps, alphabetical indexes, navigation trees that change depending on the hierarchical level are other helpful tools...:

The best is the online offer, which is clear even without all this. Then such navigation aids can be added – they are gladly accepted.

The screen is what matters: What users see on the first screen they call up is the deciding factor. The headline captivates – or not, the image appeals – or not, the sound – well, if you are not surfing without a headset while on the phone with your business partner, in an open-plan office or on public transport, you might be happy about the original background music. Many users use headphones or headsets and have shorter audio or video clips played for them.

Those who write for *smartphone screens* have to contend with particularly severe restrictions. Similar to the old *teletext, a* great deal of journalistic brevity is demanded of the news editor here. Providers of mobile TV had to learn: A football field in long shot does not come across so well on such a screen.

First things first – heeding this journalistic wisdom is vital in online journalism. Because a screen has only a limited size, it must already contain the overview of what follows in the first lines. Meaningful photos and icons support this. However, pictures alone are usually not enough – texts usually say more clearly what it is about.

No dead ends: From this follows the basic rule when linking hypertext pages: Do not create one-way streets and especially do not create dead ends, but provide *at least one* link that leads further. And allow the user to return to the initial page with *a* mouse click. These are the minimum requirements for online documents. They can be met by creating a navigation frame once. Further advice and rules for building a clear hypertext structure can be found in the chapter "Hypertext".

2.2   Terms, Forms and Formats

This article brings *terms and definitions* and describes what is meant by the *forms and formats of* online journalism. How to design and use them is shown in the following chapters.

Online offerings are primarily *non-linear:* They do not consist of a continuous text, but of several *files* that are linked to each other. Whoever writes a report on the computer for a press product, such as a magazine, usually composes *a* document, *a* file. In terms of the idea, the reader starts at the top left and stops at the end of the text, at the bottom right. Already in the printed magazine it looks different: There are infographics, text boxes with an interview, overviews and checklists. In practice, the reader skims the magazine article and gets stuck here on a subheading, there on an infographic.

From text to hypertext: You cannot read online diagonally – at least not beyond the edge of the screen. So the individual components (files), from the main text to the infographic to the interview, must be linked together in such a way that the reader has an overview of the entire offering. Instead of files, online journalism refers to individual pages – not to be confused with the content of a screen. This is merely the section of the entire page that is visible on the screen at that moment.

Site: The entire online presence of the "Spiegel", for example, comprises thousands of pages and is called a *site*. A website is therefore anything but a page (site: seat, location, place). Online products can be extensive or comprise only a few pages.

A simple online offer is structured like this: The introductory page, also called the *homepage,* contains the eye-catcher, consisting of an image, the headline and a short text (lead). In American journalism, this lead is called lead because it "leads" the article. You can observe this classic structure on the start pages of the online presences of "Spiegel" or the "Daily News" (http://www.spiegel.de, http://www.tagesschau.de).

In the simplest case, it looks like this by design:

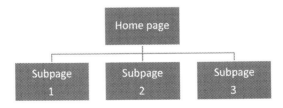

So that the users can connect to find their way through the text, the teaser is repeated on the following page.

The "Spiegel" method has a disadvantage: users have to scroll down to the next screen content to get an overview of the entire table of contents on the homepage. Many people do not do that – text that is outside the first screen is not read as often.

Therefore, the text on the homepage is shortened to the most necessary in order to draw the user into the following document, in extreme cases to a few words.

Teasers are called these "teaser words" The term originates from marketing, for example as an "incentive" in the subject of an e-mail ("You've won!"). Radio and television journalists are familiar with the teaser as a short, topic-introducing reference to subsequent broadcasts.

Teasers ensure that an introductory page is as informative as possible: they arouse curiosity, often contain the core message of the subsequent article and at the same time encourage the reader to read on.

This can be verified on the homepages of almost all media, whether http://www.t-online.de, http://www.zeit.de, http://www.sueddeutsche.de or http://www.vice.de: The first screen page always consists of several teasers. Depending on the brand character of the medium, more or less further information (in the case of tabloid media also: opinion) is already given on the introductory page. The actual article itself only follows after one or two mouse clicks.

What users can click on, is a text or image element that creates the link to the subsequent document. Because the technical distinction between text and graphics makes little sense to the user – often a graphic element looks like text – Klaus Meier has coined the term *navigation point* for both.[1] From a technical point of view, the navigation point is the jumping-off point that leads to the, hopefully accurately announced, destination.

This jump target can be within the same document – then it is called *an anchor.* The user clicks or taps to go to a destination further down, usually out of view but within the same document.

The link between the jump and the target is called a *hyperlink, or link for* short.

The term *hypertext* (Greek hyper: over, hypertext thus meaning "over text", "super text") was created for texts containing hyperlinks. It is from this term that the markup language Hypertext Markup Language HTML takes its name.

Because not only text documents are linked, we now speak of *hypermedia.* For the same reason, the term *content* has become common: not only text but also images, audio and video elements are meant. The individual elements of a page – from the button to the video file – are also called *assets.*

If a navigation point leads to a separate document within the entire online offer, the site, it is called an *internal link.*

External links lead out of the website to pages of other online providers. For strategic reasons, they are used with caution and usually rather towards the end of

---

[1] Klaus Meier (ed.), Internet Journalism (UVK, Konstanz 3rd ed. 2003).

an online contribution: After all, you want to keep the user on your own website as long as possible.

Links, whether within a page, a site or externally, are the essence of hypertext and hypermedia: They establish a network of relationships between texts, images, audio and video documents that goes beyond the capabilities of the individual provider.[2]

Like a sailor the user has to navigate through the pages by clicking or tapping. A clear structure is the be-all and end-all of a well-designed site. Similar to the sections of other media (editorial units, topic or form-bound), online providers divide their site into different topic sections or hierarchy levels. In the case of an online magazine, for example, the sections can be called lifestyle, business, family, food and drink, wellness and partnership.

Navigation between the sections within the site as easy as possible for the user should be the common goal of the online journalist as well as the screen designer.

A navigation bar consists of the texts or symbols for the individual sections of the website – as apt or "speaking" as possible. It can be hidden behind a burger symbol, have the form of tabs or resemble a table of contents, change its appearance depending on the user's action or remain as a fixed point – the main thing is that it does justice to its task of facilitating orientation and navigation. To conceptualize and plan a good web offering, create a *storyboard* before you start writing. More about the art of conception, navigation, the nature of links and how to set them can be found in the chapter "Hypertext".

What are the forms of online journalism? On the one hand, there are those forms of presentation that have been transferred from the classical media to the Internet and are now offered as hypertext:

Journalistic forms of presentation online

- *Informative* forms of presentation such as news, reports, which are up-to-date online with the shortest possible time delay, such as in the news ticker or in the livestream.
- *Narrative* forms of presentation such as reportage or interview, which often occur online in collective formats such as a dossier or a web documentary.
- *Commentary* forms of presentation such as the critique or the gloss, which frequently appear online as user contributions.
- *Advisory* or *service contributions* such as advice texts, surveys, quizzes and self-tests.
- *Also three-dimensional virtual worlds, virtual reality* as well as *augmented reality as* used by VR journalism.

---

[2] Tim Berners-Lee, The Web Report, (Econ Verlag, Munich 1999).

Content management is required for all forms and formats: planned creation and collection of data in order to make it quickly and purposefully accessible. For this purpose, editorial systems or content management systems (CMS), especially for the web sometimes also called web content management systems (WCMS), are used. They allow content to be created, edited, published and archived independently of the context in which it is used.

From static, dynamic and semi-dynamic information the content can be composed. The classic hypertext was static, as was the online archive. Today, almost all information that users compile *individually* from a database, such as "all cabaret events in the next 14 days" from an event calendar, and that is *updated* continuously at the same time, usually in automated forms, such as weather data or stock market prices, is dynamic. Semi-dynamic information is a mixture of static and dynamic elements: it is available on demand but is updated editorially, such as address databases.

Databases – that is, strictly structured information, card indexes comparable with maps and rubrics – are core components of dynamic offerings. Archives of all kinds – from photo to newspaper to film and music archives – are based on databases. Their strengths are the filtering and sorting functions as well as the ordered output of search results. They are treated under the generic term *content management*. One sometimes also speaks of "database journalism". What is meant is not the simple input of data – that is done more and more automatically. The joke is in designing and structuring such databases to make the strands of information and communication easily accessible.

The participatory forms and formats of online journalism not only use the linking of digital documents described so far, but also the special possibilities of user action and user communication that result from the combination of digital journalism and online transmission. They build on the technical possibilities offered by the medium and use them for new, online-typical forms of presentation.

The term *user-generated content* describes only a part of it, namely the share of the users, without taking into account the conceptual specifications by the editorial staff and the moderation. In other words, this is where online journalism really gets exciting.

Participatory forms and formats
(Selection, cf. the chapter of the same name):
Basically, the graduated integration of user activities (user-generated content) into an online offering. Examples:

- Crowd-based *data journalism* that engages users to mine data and generate and visualize new connections from it.
- *Blogs,* a special form of a content management system, which can be filled with different journalistic contents.
- *Microblogging services* that also act as aggregators, such as *Twitter.*
- *Photo, podcast and video platforms* and other services that combine the distribution of individually generated content (text, image, audio, video) with subscription, feedback (commentary) and other networking opportunities.
- Individual communication between users or between user and journalist via *direct message, chats, instant messenger.*
- *Inclusion of other* third-party *social media platforms or communities* such as Instagram, Facebook, Twitter, Xing or TikTok.
- Collaborative writing in *wikis (*example: Wikipedia) and indexing (*folksonomy*), also *geotagging.*

Animations can be used to visualize information as well as for commentary and caricature: the reportage online is expanded by the 360-degree panorama photo or VR reportage, the net dossier on a medical topic by a data graphic that animates statistical information. Satirical Internet formats gave rise early on to the online cartoon, an independent visual commentary form.

Streaming is the name of the technology used by live streams and web cams: Audio and video data are received and played back simultaneously in real time. On the one hand, classic radio and TV broadcast formats are transmitted via the Internet. Independent online formats have emerged. Internet radio and online TV stations have been added, often extended by participative, collaborative production. Data is compressed for mobile devices.

Provide these media formats for download (download) is the bandwidth-saving alternative to streaming. The user can then listen to or watch them *time-delayed.* The Internet merely serves as a transport medium.

To answer the user's questions, is also one of the tasks of the online journalist. Not only that he usually receives corrections, opinions and suggestions from direct user contact, not only that he (more often) is an advisor himself, – in addition, the quick and easy communication by mail is also the best guarantee for user site loyalty.

If several forms of presentation and media are linked, we talk about online formats in this book. Communities thrive on the exchange of opinions, the value of a newsletter lies in the quality of the advice it gives (advice or service journalism), the newsroom of an online magazine leaves the expression of opinions to the users. Weblogs often consist of comments.

Online formats

- Onepager and "scrollytelling", which combine different forms of presentation and media on a single, very long page on a single topic.
- Topic dossiers and webdocs that combine contributions from different media and from different forms of presentation in a more comprehensive online offering from several websites.
- *Mashups* that combine such services with traditional forms.

Between synchronous and asynchronous forms is also helpful in the classification. Chat and dynamic pages belong to the synchronous or "live" forms, blogs, podcasts or media libraries to the time-delayed, asynchronous forms.

Advertising and editorial contributions are clearly separated: this is required by journalism ethics, but it is also in the interest of the user's own credibility: the user notices when a book review in an apparently independent online magazine is merely intended to encourage him to click on the book order, and the credibility of the text drops. With an online bookshop, on the other hand, the user is not surprised by this connection. Transparency is therefore called for: through clear labelling ('our partner in the online book trade: Amazon') or the simple reference 'Display'.

2.3   Workflow and Content Management

Project management and modern communication systems are indispensable for an online editorial team that wants to exchange content with authors and content brokers on the one hand, and with users and business partners on the other.

In the efficient bundling of resources personnel, material and time help software packages. As difficult as it is, do not let the software dictate your workflows; instead, define the workflow together in the online editorial team. The software product you then choose must not only enable these organizational processes, but make them transparent. Otherwise, you can go right back to the pegboard.

Regular team meetings help plan beyond the day. A glance at the shared diary shows what the coming week, the next month will bring: Deutsche Telekom AG's balance sheet press conference, the publication of the latest labour market figures, the opening of a new Internet department store. Seasonal themes and seasonal "holes" can be integrated into theme plans. Unforeseen things happen anyway ...

On-air or *page criticism* – terms that have been transferred from traditional editorial departments – is a permanent feature of online editorial teams. If possible, a different member of the editorial team analyzes the current online edition and comments on the structure, text and image design as well as the linking.

Monitoring is a tool for evaluating the position of one's own editorial team within the media landscape. This means observing and commenting on the products of comparable online offerings based on objective evaluation criteria.

Stylebook or style guide contain the editorial specifications for text and design. They ensure a smooth workflow and transparency. The rules or *guide-lines* provide specifications for the textual (e.g. editorial agreements) and graphic design (e.g. typeface, colour), for example for teasers, headlines, leads, body text, templates and metadata, but also for images and captions.

In the marketing field, a stylebook or style guide additionally conveys the underlying mission statement, the communication goals and the core messages.

Short decision-making processes, flat information hierarchies help when things do get tight with the schedule. Murphy's law applies inexorably: Whatever can go wrong, will go wrong. It is good to have substitute solutions ready for the most important cases. Editor-in-chief on vacation, CvD in hospital: Can the online editor who is left alone in the editorial office release news? Can he access all the information he needs? Or is the central information stored securely on the boss's computer?

The editorial archive no longer comprises only the published articles. Communication with suppliers (authors, content brokers, etc.) as well as with users should be managed electronically and released for joint access. Names, addresses, telephone numbers and e-mail addresses must be available to the entire editorial team.

Content repository is the name of this digital filing system. It can be organized as a file system, a database or a mixture of both and manages the *assets*. These are the individual components of a website that make up the content: text, image, sound or video files. For each asset, you record who created it, when it was created, and when and where it was used. This *meta-information* belongs together with the assets in the content repository. In the course of editorial work, assets are conceived, produced and filed. The *content life cycle* describes the stages that an asset passes through from its conception to its archiving.

Database concepts are behind all editorial systems. They assume that information can be structured – evident with addresses, less visible with contact information (who knows an expert for cat breeding?), difficult to implement with full-text data volumes. Here only concise abstracts of each text in the database help, journalistically speaking: Lead texts. At least these *abstracts* must be searchable as full text. A stopgap solution are *keywords* that describe the content as precisely as possible and, above all, make it retrievable. Searching audio and video material is also feasible – it just takes longer.

Data journalism: Bundling and evaluating database information is no longer the task of the online journalist. Smart apps take over this task. With one exception: the journalist still has to ask the questions about the data sets. Programming skills and a basic understanding of structured information as well as knowledge of statistical methods are an advantage.

Robot journalism is a somewhat unfortunate name for automated text production. Internationally, the terms *automated journalism, algorithmic journalism* or *machine-written journalism* are common. A database is fed with a lot of structured text. If it now receives appropriately structured new data, for example about a football match, it uses an algorithm to compile a sports report containing the essential facts – if desired, even from the perspective of one team or the other. Print and online editorial teams have been working with this for a long time. The more information is added, the more the system learns. The next step is automated video production of standardizable content.

"As with data journalism or research with large amounts of data *(Big Data)*, the journalist is increasingly supported or partially replaced by the computer in robot journalism," writes journalism professor Markus Kaiser. He also reports on tests to have the software independently search for further information online in addition to the given structured data on the topic, in order to incorporate it into the texts.

Editorial system, content management system (CMS) or web content management system (WCMS) – the terms are used for mini to giant systems for online publication. The correct term in the online sector is *web content management system* (WCMS) – but even here the shortened term CMS has become common. Regardless of the designation, the software solutions differ in the scope of performance, sometimes considerably.

Decision criteria for an editorial system

- What document management and asset management options does the CMS offer?
- Which external tools (editors) can be integrated?
- The scalability: Which script languages does the CMS support? Which web techniques are supported?
- How can additional formats be integrated? Does the CMS process standard formats via which it can import and export data, such as HTML or XML?
- Project and workflow management: How does it handle access control, the release cycle, to-do lists and status reports?
- System-specific data such as server platform, supported web server and supported database systems

Test possibilities, reference customers, price.

Knowledge management means nothing other than: Information is merely the raw material. What matters is its procurement, processing and availability: Is exactly the information that each editor needs available at the right time?

In organisational terms, the problems are similar whether you are an online editor in a service company such as a bank or insurance company, work for a church or trade union, for a mass medium with an online presence, or work for an online editorial office "pure and simple".

Content for whom? In almost all editorial offices, one has to deal with the triad *intranet – extranet – internet,* which takes place under the common browser-operated HTML or XML surface:

Intranet, extranet, internet

- *Intranet* refers to a closed network of a precisely defined number of users: the employees of one's own company. They have their own access rights (accounts) and, depending on the department to which they belong, have graduated reading and writing rights. In editorial contexts, all publishing house employees participate in the intranet with different rights, from marketing to the editorial department to the human resources department.
- *Extranet* extends the circle of authorized users to include external employees or sales partners. In the case of an editorial office, the external editorial offices and correspondents are integrated into the extranet; in the case of an association or institution, perhaps the voluntary employees (in addition to the full-time employees who use the intranet) or the full-time members of other regional associations. In globally operating companies, the extranet integrates in particular the sales force – in the case of insurance companies also: the independent insurance brokers. Characteristic here is also a password-protected access to a defined area, often separated according to read and write authorization. This means, for example: One person is allowed to read everything the others write, but he is not allowed to interfere with their texts.
- *Internet* refers to the totality of online publication possibilities par excellence, accessible to every user. What is written here is publicly readable. The writing permission for users is limited. A final edit for everything that goes online is recommended.

The target groups differ not only organizationally according to access authorization. When selecting content, it makes a significant difference whether information is prepared for colleagues from the same company, for cooperation partners in the USA or for the user somewhere out there. In any case, you need online journalistic skills as described in the previous chapters.

Content types. *Dynamic* pages, which automatically change their content, are in contrast to purely static offers. Every hypertext offer is initially *static:* it presents itself to the user in the same form until the online journalist changes something about it. Compiling the city portal's calendar of events would thus become a time-consuming activity for the journalist. But also for the user: he would have to scroll through mountains of event tips until he finally found the jazz concerts he was looking for. Here a date database on the server helps, from which with the help of an input mask the desired can be sorted out after several characteristics – for instance period and genre – fast. The provider obtains the event data automatically from a content supplier, who ensures regular updates. After starting the search query, all that appears on the user's screen are all the jazz concerts that have been announced for Thursday to Saturday.

Semi-dynamic information is a mixture of static and dynamic elements: it is available on demand, but is updated editorially. Stock market prices, product shopping baskets, but also cooking recipes or consumer tips can be compiled from strictly structured databases in an up-to-date and individual way. Further examples: the price development of the Microsoft share over the course of the last week – or all cooking recipes in which Jerusalem artichoke is used.

Personalize web content requires dynamic concepts in user management. The result is individual text offers of the online magazine, specifically tailored to the interests of the user, or *personal radio* with the favorite titles of each individual: The system has "remembered" the user's preferences.

Content from where? The journalistic procurement of information from sources such as agency material, own research as well as from archives and libraries is one of the basics of journalistic training.[3] It would be a mistake to believe that online journalists only do research online – this is just as nonsensical as the assertion that radio journalists must primarily listen to the radio for research and that daily newspaper journalists only read other newspapers. Online journalists make phone calls, read printed press releases and conduct on-site interviews just like any other journalist.

Moreover, online research also allows various ways of obtaining information: original sources can be found online, ideas arise from user contact, contacts can be

---

[3] La Roche's Einführung in den praktischen Journalismus (Journalistische Praxis) (Journalistische Praxis), Wiesbaden: Springer VS, 20th Aufl. 2017.

established, agency reports, archives and databases are available – including a great deal of journalistically prepared information.

Research and counter-research. It goes without saying that online journalists should be well versed in online research. Textbooks on this exist.[4] In addition, they should know and use the methods of classic journalistic research. In times of content partnerships and other cooperations, it is especially important to hear the other side (*audiatur et altera pars*).[5]

Take over information? There is a great deal of uncertainty – not only among online journalists – regarding the legal situation: Can I simply take over content from other providers that would fit well into my offering?

The answer is a bit more complicated, it is: Copyright law of course also applies online, see chapter "The law". And it says clearly: ideas as well as the information content are not protectable.

You can therefore safely take over information that you find online if you formulate it yourself. However, you bear all the consequences if the simple report, which you have taken unseen from the news offer of another online magazine, turns out to be a false report. The *source reference* (As the industry service XY reports ...), supported by a hyperlink, therefore has its purpose.

With completely prepared content it looks completely different: You can only take over complete text contributions, photos, audio and video if you have clarified the rights with the licensor (see also chapter "The right").

There is one exception to this rule: Press information of all kinds, which companies and institutions place on the web marked as such, is intended for further use. Increasingly, you will find not only texts and statistics, photos and charts, but also original sounds and videos.

If you now have the phrase "You must always listen to the other side" in your ear, almost nothing can happen: Next to the jubilant ad hoc announcement about how much the company's share price has risen (original quote from the CEO), place the announcement from the industry service that no investor can be found.

Agencies and brokers provide information that is appropriate to the market segment. Media companies have to pay for the fact that the contributions can be adopted 1:1. The German Press Agency (dpa), for example, supplies words, photos, graphics, audio and video. The largest German agency supplies news from all departments (politics, business, culture, sport, miscellaneous). For news offerings

---

[4] Some examples: Klaus Meier (ed.): Internet-Journalismus, Konstanz: UVK 2002, 3rd ed.; Stefan Karzauninkat: Die Suchfibel, Leipzig: Klett Schulbuch-Verlag 2008; Markus Kaiser, Recherchieren (Journalistische Praxis) Wiesbaden: Springer VS 2015.
[5] La Roche a.a.O.

on the Internet, dpa has developed its own service, dpa-online. There are also information services tailored to target groups for customers who do not belong to the media industry.

Major agencies with their online presences: Deutsche Presse-Agentur at http://www.dpa.de, Agence France Presse (AFP) at http://www.afp.com, Associated Press (AP) at http://www.ap.org, Reuters at http://www.reuters.de.

Portals, catalogues and search engines also occasionally act as content brokers. Information from all over the world is provided by the automatically compiled news overview from Google (http://news.google.de) or Bing (http://www.bing.com/news). The media companies themselves act as content sellers, such as Burda with Focus digital.

Branding: If your own online editorial team is planning to enter the market as a content broker, more marketing than journalistic knowledge is required: Which market segment do you cover? What competition do you have to reckon with? What is the brand character of your product? Does it damage the image of your online product if it appears in this or that context? If there is any: Preserve the brand character of the parent medium (*one brand/all media*).

Among the most popular content, The services that can be booked online include general news, stock market and financial information, horoscopes and weather reports. But also specialized information from the media and computer industry, from medicine and other sciences, from art and literature are available online, even complete guidebook and e-learning products.

Content syndication is the buzzword for content trading. For those who find it too inconvenient to compile content themselves from the various providers, content shops take on this task as a service. They have the content delivered by dpa, afp or special services such as Wallstreet Online and compile it individually for the customer according to his requirements. They take care of the rights (digital rights management) as well as the technical implementation (encoding, hosting, interfaces). This model has a future as streaming content syndication, especially for *audio and video* content.

The acquisition of partnerships and cooperations is also part of the business of online journalists at some media companies. As a rule, turnover-based commissions are paid. Anyone working in this field needs at least a good commercial nose – but a business education does not hurt either.

Technical knowledge, on the other hand, is necessary, to design the implementation of the content partnership. It is particularly important that the interfaces are correct: between the format in which the data is submitted and the format in which it is implemented. In many houses, this is not the task of the online journalists, but of the webmasters.

As before, the acquisition of advertisements traditionally is located in the marketing department. Online editors who directly participate in the sales of a product they present in the editorial section can read up on the German Press Council's view of surreptitious advertising: At http://www.presserat.de, journalistic virtues and vices are compiled in an easy-to-read manner with practical examples.

Create transparency. The demand for a separation of editorial and advertising sections is almost more difficult to enforce online than in radio or TV broadcasts. Where the exact dividing line is between "cooperation" and "paid advertisement" can often only be determined in individual cases.

One criterion: Does the advertiser influence the content to the extent that biased information is provided, for example disguised as consumer information, which would not otherwise be published? Another: Is the cooperation transparent for the user? If a discussion forum in the online edition of a women's magazine on the subject of losing weight, which is sponsored by a margarine manufacturer, is called "Lätta-Forum", this is certainly the case – the tips on losing weight available there can still be independent and helpful from the manufacturer. (This manual does not deal with questions of trademark and competition law).

Also designations such as "XY-Online-Shop" make it clear that sales are being made here. Annoying for the user are sites that claim to offer information for senior citizens, for example – and advertise relevant products editorially on every page. The credibility of such "magazines" is correspondingly low. Lutz Frühbrodt has written a critical study on the non-transparent mimicry of content marketing vis-à-vis specialist journalistic portals.[6]

---

[6] Lutz Frühbrodt: Content Marketing. How "corporate journalists" influence public opinion. Frankfurt am Main: Otto Brenner Foundation 2016.

Abstract

The chapter describes user research methods and explains the basics of search engine optimization (SEO).

How many online users are there? What do they do online? What are users looking for online? The question of whether someone is online or offline can be safely shelved in 2020. According to the latest figures from the ARD-ZDF Online Study (2019), more than 90% of German citizens are regularly online. But since the spread of smartphones, everyone is online anyway – the distinction has all but disappeared.

Nevertheless, the following applies in principle: Anyone who offers online content must deal with their target groups. "All interested citizens" is too imprecise. Who is the web offer aimed at? What is to be communicated? Only then can the online offer be planned and designed, only then can one decide how content must be formulated and prepared so that it also reaches the target group.

The conception of a journalistic online offering includes a market and target group analysis in advance. This results in considerations about content, structure and layout. Once the offer is online, key figures such as *page impressions (PI)* and *visits* help to identify user structures and preferences.

Information and communication are what users seek most: "More than 80 % of users said they used search engines", closely followed by writing e-mails. More than 50 % still said they "search for specific offers in a targeted manner". Internet use differs greatly by age group: According to the ARD-ZDF study, almost all young people between 14 and 19 are online. Even among the over 70s, it is just under a third.

Mobile internet access is currently (2019) around 80% of mobile phone owners, according to a study by industry association Bitkom. At least 57 million Germans use a smartphone. Parallel to this, the sales figures for MP3 players, digital cameras or navigation devices are declining.

Where to get such numbers and how they come about, this chapter first describes. The section "Being found with search engines" builds on this.

3.1   User Research and Market Analysis

How many people currently use the Internet? Before we quickly quote a number such as "around four billion" or "around 50% of the world's population", we need to ask: How can they be counted at all? Who should be counted – everyone who has access to the Internet in some way, people with their own email address, or just those who have their own computer?

About the number of actual users, who have access to the Internet via such a host can only be estimated on the basis of surveys. "The art of estimating how many are online throughout the world is an inexact one at best," is how the information service *Nua Internet Surveys* describes the state of affairs. It defines "Internet user" as a person with Internet access – which is significantly more than those who have their own paid Internet access (account). As with most statistical surveys, definitions are first made and then representative samples are evaluated. This is how the market research institute Nielsen, the International Telecommunications Union (ITU) or the Society for Consumer Research work. If you are interested in an answer to the question posed at the beginning: The website http://internetworldstats.com evaluates the available sources.

Exact figures due to the way the Internet is organized, the technology only provides information on the number of *domain addresses* registered. *Denic* (Deutsche Network Information Center eG, http://www.denic.de), a cooperative, is responsible for the Federal Republic. It is one of many national companies that administer domain addresses. Denic is a good source if you want to know who is behind a web address with the ending .de. For data protection reasons, however, you must first prove that you have a legitimate interest in this information, for example because you have claims against someone.

Internationally, the *Internet Corporation for Assigned Names and Numbers* (ICANN), a non-profit organization, has been coordinating Internet administration up to now. It is gradually handing over the administration of domains to private companies such as Verisign.

Under the name "W3B Surveys" the consultancy Fittkau & Maaß regularly conducts online surveys. The survey examines socio-demographic structures, general media usage habits, the use of print media and TV stations online, as well as the wishes, opinions and assessments of online users on topics such as advertising, online shopping and online financial services. The sampling basis is all persons who are online and participate in the survey within the 6-week survey period. The sample size depends on the number of participating World Wide Web users and has been increasing continuously since the first W3B survey in 1995 (http://www.w3b. de).

In classical media research online usage is being included more and more. The ARD "Media Basic Data", a joint project of the specialist journal "Media Perspectives" and SWR Media Research, provides information on programming and media usage in all media sectors in Germany for online research (http://www. media-perspektiven.de). In addition to information on media offerings and media use, the range of topics also includes data on the technical reception situation and the media industry in Germany. Here, the socio-demographics of online users, times, duration and location of online use as well as the actual online usage options are recorded in a differentiated manner.

On-site and telephone surveys on online reach have been conducted by the *Arbeitsgemeinschaft Media-Analyse e. V.* (http://www.agma-mmc.de) since 2004.

The industry association Bitkom calls itself "Germany's digital association". It regularly collects market data, including labour market and economic data, and also conducts user research (http://www.bitkom.de).

Into the field of vision of journalism and communication science since the mid-1990s, the Internet has become the focus of numerous media-specific studies, cf. the current research projects at the Leibniz Institute for Media Research – Hans Bredow Institute (http://www.hans-bredow-institut.de) or the studies by Christoph Neuberger, Münster. A good place to start: the specialist group on *digital communication* at the *German Society for Journalism and Communication Studies* (DGPuK).

Online call-off figures have a comparable function to determining circulation figures or paid circulation in the press: This is used to determine the advertising media performance of online media. Since 1997, the Information Association for the Determination of the Distribution of Advertising Media (*Informationsgemeinschaft zur Feststellung der Verbreitung von Werbeträgern* – IVW) has published monthly call-up figures for online media that voluntarily submit to this procedure. Technically, this is done using counting software that collects and evaluates the data. It uses the ability of each web server to log the accesses to the individual pages in so-called *logfiles* ("logbook files").

The so-called hits, accesses to the individual files, the server-side program counts in the simplest case. An HTML page can consist of one or many files – depending on how many graphic or other media elements are used. Example: A user clicks on the homepage, which consists of 18 small graphics and four text files – one page, many hits. Therefore, more meaningful metrics than hits were created.

Page impressions and visits: However, the number of hits on the company logo or a navigation button, for example, is not very meaningful. Therefore, only the so-called *page impressions* (PI), the accesses to the HTML pages themselves, are counted. They indicate the number of visual contacts of users with an HTML page. For offers with frames, only the first access to a frameset counts as PI.

The longer a user spends on a website, the more pages he views and the longer he *stays.* Such a coherent usage process or visit is called a *visit* (also: *unique visit*). According to IVW, it defines the advertising medium contact. Every website provider can obtain the above-mentioned statistical data from his provider and evaluate it using a suitable tool.

For dynamic offers, which are currently generated from databases, this measurement is also of no help. For this purpose, IVW has developed a time-based measurement method: How long is a certain dynamic content visible for a certain number of users *(user minutes)?*

Distortions in the collection of call-off figures are caused by the fact that web offers on the Internet are temporarily stored on so-called *proxy servers* and retrieved from there. These and other methodological difficulties and how they affect the measurements are described by IVW on its site (http://www.ivw.de).

3.2   Being Found with Search Engines

The most popular search engine in Germany is currently (as of 2020) *Google* with just under 95%. *Bing,* the second most popular, only has a market share of just over 4 percent. If you want to be found on the Internet with a web offer, you cannot get around Google.

How often other sites link to a particular page, Google was the first search engine to include: What many find good cannot be completely wrong. The result is striking: Google almost always delivers excellent results from halfway trustworthy sources. Anyone who writes for the Internet must therefore make sure that their texts are found via Google.

How Google works exactly, is ultimately, as with any search engine, a trade secret. However, the company gives all sorts of advice under the heading "Google for webmasters", what helps to a good *ranking* on the first places and what not. To be among the first ten hits on Google is quite a good ranking. Only, what term are people searching for? When the author of this book searches Google for her name, she finds herself at the top – no mean feat. After all, how much competition will there be for that name? And more importantly, who else is going to search for "Hooffacker"? In my case, it would be much more interesting to see that when people search for "online journalism", the website for this book is in the top ten hits. This varies from individual to individual, since the search results are personalized – try it out.

Can you buy Google? No, the publisher has not paid for the fact that this book occasionally appears at the top of the Google hits. However, they do pay for the fact that certain hits, slightly differentiated by colour, are at the top of the list. That is why the word *advertisement is* placed above these hits. The same applies to the results on the right-hand side of the page. Behind this is a Google advertising option using keywords called *Adwords,* cf. http://adwords.google.com.

How to get listed among the first ten hits on Google, on the other hand, is a craft in which text plays a major role. It goes by the name of *Search Engine Optimization (SEO).*

Search engine optimization is not witchcraft. Search engines like Google try to map the reading behavior of users with their rating algorithms. To do this, they make use of various auxiliary constructions. Does a term appear not only once on a web page, but more often? Is it more likely to be at the top of the list? Does the term searched for perhaps even appear in the headline? If there are several terms that are being searched for: Are these terms close together rather than far apart? Is the page updated from time to time? All of these – in addition to good linking – are signs to a search engine that the web page in question is fairly relevant to the term being searched for.

The search engines differ in how they weight the individual criteria. Therefore, they deliver slightly different search results. Websites change constantly, and so does the ranking – that is why you can never rest too long on the laurels of a one-time good ranking.

How does a search engine work? The basis of every search engine is a fairly large database. The database is created by a program, a *crawler* or *robot, which* searches the World Wide Web. As soon as it finds a link to another page, it follows it and also includes the new page in its inventory. The content of the page is evaluated for the index. When you make a search query, it does not search "the Internet", but only the index.

This has already made it clear that no search engine fully represents "the Internet". It always knows only a section. In addition, there are areas that are not visible to search engines. The so-called *darknet is one* of them.

The search engines generally perform a full-text search. This means that all words that appear on the web pages are included and indexed. Anyone who types one of these words into their search query will also receive a reference to this page at some point.

Most of the time it is not even necessary to register your own website with the search engine – which costs nothing and is quite easy. But making sure that the robot or spider of the search engine or catalog finds your own homepage during its routine tours through the web is only the first step.

Numerous myths surround search engine optimization. Since the search engines' business model is to deliver advertising that is as individually tailored as possible, they try to find the best possible answer for users. In the process, the secret is quickly unraveled: Writing for search engines means writing for users. And that is where the journalistic craft helps:

- know your own target group,
- identify current issues and content,
- use common terms and appropriate verbs,
- use the lexical variance (i.e. "Wire bike" instead of "Bicycle") with restraint,
- be active in several media and cross-link from one to the other.

More on this topic can be found in the chapter "Forms of presentation".

Text counts. In order for the beautiful animations, graphics, audios and videos to be found by search engines, they need speaking description texts. Search engine programmers are working on evaluating image and AV files. But up to now, in the case of images, audio or video podcasts, it is mainly the text and keywords that are taken into account, in addition to the degree of linking. Nevertheless, the use of image or video improve the ranking.

In addition, there are some simple things that need to be considered technically.

How do you get a new term into Google? To test this, the German computer magazine c't called a search engine optimization contest in April 2005. The aim was to achieve the best position in certain search engines, including Google, on two key dates, May 15 and December 15. *Hommingberger Gepardenforelle* was chosen as the term because there is neither a place called *Hommingberg* nor a *cheetah trout*. From the top ten winners, some valid strategies for getting found can still be derived today, even though the rules for ranking are constantly changing.

Does the term appear in the URL? The *domain name* plays an essential role. http://www.hommingberger-gepardenforelle.de was always amongst the first ten hits. But also http://de.wikipedia.org/wiki/Hommingberger_Gepardenforelle had good cards. Instead of using file names like 12345.html, you should give the individual pages meaningful URLs, as many content management systems (CMS) now do.

A meaningful domain address is the be-all and end-all. It is good to get hold of meaningful addresses such as http://www.zeit.de, http://www.spiegel.de, http://www.frauenbund.de or http://www.verbraucherzentrale.de at an early stage. People can remember such words better than http://www.vzbv.de or http://www.kdfb.de. If you only have such an address, you would be well advised to define a more comprehensible address for yourself.

The gist is in the title. This technical *title* is not identical to the title of the post on the website. You can find it if you look in the blue status bar at the top of your browser. Most CMS allow you to enter this title manually. If the term you are looking for appears here, it will be given priority in the ranking. If you only have "Home", there is a need for action.

What is behind all this? Web pages are written using a standard language called HTML and are divided into a visible part (body) and an invisible part (head). Let us take a look at the HTML or source code of any page: In the header or "head" of the HTML document, you will always find a line that starts with <title> and ends with </title>. All these commands in angle brackets are called "tag" (plural: tags). We would like to draw your attention to what is in between: because this line is evaluated preferentially by the search engines.

Suppose a company offers seminars on time and project management. Then not only the word "seminar" should appear in the title, but also an appropriate keyword for the content of the seminars, for example "time management". The robot evaluates these keywords and the search engine takes them into account when ranking.

Does the term appear in the title? In HTML code, headings are also marked with a "tag". The search engine weights what is between heading tags higher than plain text. An apt, journalistically formulated headline therefore also helps with search engine optimization. The same applies to bold print (also recognizable to the search engine by HTML tags), image captions and the so-called alternative tags that are displayed for images when you move the mouse pointer over them.

Fodder for the database: Meta keywords. You can also provide the search engine database with specific information about the authors and the content. We have already learned about the title tag. In addition, there are tags that define what can be directly transferred to the database, so-called meta tags. Stefan Karzauninkat, author of the "Search Primer", provides an overview of the most important tags (http://www.suchfibel.de).

Caution, trap: Google does not like it when you enter keywords as keywords in the metatags that have nothing to do with the text!

How do you find the right keywords? The best way to do this is to put yourself in the shoes of someone searching for a specific topic. But you can also simply observe the habits of your users: What search terms do they use and in what combination? Do they tend to search for "car" or for "automotive"? Google helps here too with the most common search terms or a trend analysis that lets you compare two or more terms (http://trends.google.de).

In which context do search terms occur? Which other words have a semantic relationship to the term? If you want to generate advertising success via Google Adwords, you will find tips and tools for finding the right terms.

The fact that a website can be used on mobile devices is also an important technical requirement for a good ranking. In addition, there is the speed of the website, also in mobile search, and increasingly the optimization for voice assistants.

Tools and toolbars. Google, Yahoo and others provide free online *tools* to examine websites for their potential. These include browser add-ons called toolbars, which are easy to install. The one from Google is available at http://toolbar.google.com. This makes it easy to test how a website compares to the competition online. Google provides other competitive analysis tools under the name Google Analytics (http://www.google.com/analytics). From "Seobility" to "Yoast" to "Screaming frog": Since the terms of use often change, it is best to research online for current SEO tools.

If you want to make topics or products ensure the appropriate keyword density on special *landing pages*. Such a page catches the user and offers him suitable further actions. This is usually not necessary for a journalistic text contribution: If authors take the rules for good journalistic texts to heart, call a spade a spade and find apt headlines, search engine optimization almost results by itself. However, you can also call the whole thing *"editorial search engine optimization"* (ESEO) and do it in a targeted manner.

Using social networks can also be called *"social media optimization"* – and if it goes well, also *"viral marketing"* online. This takes advantage of the fact that good or funny content spreads online almost by itself: through the users. The collective indexing with *hashtags,* named after the double cross # "hash" as well as after the keywords "tags" also called tagging, provides traffic as well as corresponding blog entries. Since bloggers are networked through links, backlinks, trackbacks, good links spread quickly. Twitter can be used to disseminate information in short form, including URLs or their abbreviated version, the TinyURLs.

Podcasts to listen to and watch also support search engine optimisation, provided they are well written and keyworded. Above all, search engines evaluate people's relationships via *social media*.

Whether it's a website, blog entry, image or podcast- the above tips apply to all media. With the photo or graphic, the alternative text is important, but also the caption. Podcasts, whether audio or video, need a fitting text description, a search engine optimized written teaser. For all social media applications, keywording is essential.

Links are considered recommendations. Because search engines rank better ("PageRank", named after Larry Page) if you have many links to your own site, many website owners make intensive efforts to establish link partnerships with sites that have a good ranking. Link exchange and reciprocal linking are legitimate ways to use one's own network profitably.

Caution, trap: If the linked pages have little to do with each other thematically, Google thinks linking is a trick. The same applies to the formerly popular method of artificially generating links to one's own site. Resourceful providers use sites invented purely for this purpose – after all, it costs nothing to link to your own pages.

Google also does not like it when multiple URLs point to the same (mirrored) content.

Search engines expose tricks. Most of these tricks only help in the short term. The programmers of the robots and the rankings for the search engines also observe what the providers of websites are up to and craft countermeasures for it.

Stefan Karzauninkat, the author of the "Search Primer", notes somewhat annoyed: "Quite a few smart alecks try to spur the search engines on to top performance with the aim of presenting their own page as first as possible in the list of search results". But that does not help: "In the meantime, such pages are relegated to the bottom of the list or not even included in the index".

What if Google does not like a site anymore? On this point, the power of a large search engine can quickly become very unpleasant: If Google has the impression that a site is working with unfair methods, it is sometimes taken out completely. The site is then no longer findable for users who search with Google.

Further Reading

1. Wiebke Möhring, Daniela Schlütz: Die Befragung in der Medien- und Kommunikationswissenschaft. Eine praxisorientierte Einführung, Wiesbaden: Springer VS 2019
2. Julian Dziki: Suchmaschinenoptimierung für Dummies. Weinheim: Wiley-VCH 2018

Further Links

3. Google für Webmaster: https://www.google.com/webmasters/
4. Google Trends: https://www.google.com/trends/
5. Google Analytics: https://www.google.com/analytics/

Hypertext and Storyboard

4

Abstract

This chapter provides practical guidance on designing for online use: How do I write hypertext? How do I ensure user-friendly navigation, how do I write a storyboard for the site?

In the simplest case, **hypertext begins with** a short text that links to a subsequent page with text, audio, video or another file element. Longer articles require *structuring with the help of links*. Thematically related dossiers or entire online magazines in turn require a clear hypertext structure. Therefore, this chapter starts with the smallest unit and then gradually approaches the complete online offering.

The first article is dedicated to the writing of hypertext – from the short summary (lead) to the fitting headline (head) to the teaser. How to structure a longer text clearly is described in the following article "Links structure the reading flow". Structuring an online magazine and navigation are the topics of the next article "Storyboard for navigation". There you will also find tips for the design of the start page as well as for the more extensive forms on the web, from dossiers to online magazines.

4.1   How to Write Hypertext?

How do you write for online media? Should we even talk about "writing" anymore, or is "designing" or "communication design" the more appropriate term? I prefer the term "write" to make it clear: In the beginning, there is still the word.

© Springer Fachmedien Wiesbaden GmbH, part of Springer Nature 2022
G. Hooffacker, *Online journalism*,
https://doi.org/10.1007/978-3-658-35731-3_4

First and foremost, words serve as orientation online. The fact that online journalists have to think visually (where is the user looking?) and interactively (what is the user doing?) does not contradict this. For pictograms and graphics as navigation aids, a context must first be established in which they are valid.

How much words shape our perception, is illustrated by the Stroop effect. In the 1930s, the American psychologist J. Ridley Stroop tested the perception and reproduction behavior of readers when the text offered sent contradictory signals. He asked: How does the colouring of the typeface influence the perception of the word content? Specifically: If the word "blue" is printed in green – what is the user reading?

Try it out: At http://www.kommdesign.de, communication psychologist Thomas Wirth has put up an impressive demonstration of the Stroop effect. The user gets stuck when he has to name the color of the words printed in a different color. The word "blue", printed in green, arrives at the user as "blue". Stroop has already identified the superimposition (interference) of two processes, namely "reading" and "naming the color", as the cause of this effect. Such interference not only distracts the user, but can cause him to abort the reading process and click away. Online at http://www.kommdesign.de/texte/stroop.htm you can try out the Stroop effect for yourself and draw your own conclusions.

The Stroop effect is not an argument against images – quite the contrary: Of course, photos and graphics are not only excellent eye-catchers, but ideally provide information that text could only convey with a delay or at great expense. But even images without explanatory words leave the viewer perplexed: text must be. And if image and text contradict each other in their message, the resulting interference can irritate the user to such an extent that he leaves the page. Or even worse: The images prevent the user from concentrating on the (complex) text.

An example of successful use of text is Google with its simple home page, the aim of which is to provide quick orientation for the user. But text also provides the basic orientation aid online across the media: for photo pages, audio sequences and even film and video. And text supports your findability on Google.

Hypertext is the form that is most closely related to classic text of all online formats. Here there is a clear separation between sender and receiver. The user perceives the text time-delayed, asynchronously. But that is where the similarities end. There is still a vague similarity between magazine and online texts: The magazine page already highlights blocks of text with the help of the layout and offers opportunities for cross-entry. Teaser texts on the front page are intended to encourage the reader to continue reading inside and to buy the magazine.

To be continued! The simplest hypertext application could be reduced to this denominator. All editors of press products use it when they reproduce an article from a daily newspaper or magazine one-to-one online. Because the text is in any case too long for the homepage (after all, other topics are also to be referred to there), it is merely touched on or "teased".

How to write a hypertext message? The following information is an excerpt from http://www.spiegel.de. Please read through the text and think about: Which information would absolutely have to appear in an announcement text, and which could be dispensed with? What headline would you write for it?

(dpa) In Bavaria, a freight train rolled unbraked on its way out of the Bohemian Forest towards Wiesau in the Upper Palatinate. The driver of a private train company had signalled to the staff in the signal box that there was no braking effect and asked for help, said a spokesman for Deutsche Bahn.

An accident had been prevented because of the quick reaction of several dispatchers along the line. They adjusted the signals on the line in such a way that the train was finally able to roll out and come to a halt after more than 80 km.

Why the train failed to brake when it ran down the slightly sloping track last Thursday is under investigation. (abridged).

Practical exercise to play along: Please compose a message that filters out the essentials from this information, of 250 characters or less. Please check the length with the function "Count words" in the menu "Tools" of Word.

The seven journalistic W-questions will help you solve the task:

Who
(does) *something*
when
where
as
why
from where

That way you know what absolutely belongs in the message. In our example, this simple checklist might look like this:

Who freight train
(does) rolls
when (August 2019)
where through Bavaria
as if unchecked
why human error
where (did the information come from)? dpa

Spiegel online knitted its headline from these answers at the time:

((Roof line)) Allegedly more than 100 km/h
((Headline)) Freight train rolls unbraked through Bavaria
((Lead)) In Bavaria, the brakes failed on a freight train: the locomotive and the wagons rolled unbraked for dozens of kilometres towards the Danube valley.

Pretty dramatic, right? But is that really the news core? The answers could also look like this:

Who railwayman
(does) *what* prevent train crash
when (August 2019)
where Upper Palatinate
how with quick reaction
why train rolled more than 80 km, brakes had failed
where (did the information come from)? dpa.

n-tv has opted for this solution:

((Roof line)) Serious accident prevented
((Headline)) Freight train steers unbraked through Bavaria
((Lead)) The train drivers apply the brakes, but their train does not slow down: a freight train from the Czech Republic does not come to a stop until many miles from its destination. Now the authorities are investigating.

In **the selection of information** different strategies become clear: "inform" versus "arouse curiosity". Especially since daily media hide their articles behind a paywall, they use the curiosity teasers. This is unsatisfactory for users because the teaser does not fully convey the core of the news.

Preparing a message for the screen means above all: finding out what is essential, what is current, what is special. To do this, you need some knowledge – namely about what is new for your target group in this information, and what is already known. And you need to know who you are writing for.

How do you write a good teaser? Please try it out for yourself: What could such a teaser look like?

If you want to solve the task in front of your PC, please write a short text of no more than 120 characters and a heading of no more than six words. Please check the length of the text with word's "word count" function. If you are over 180 characters, please seriously check what information you could do without.

After a moment's thought, you may have written something that looks like the following text in the headline – teaser – message sequence.

((Roof line)) Quick response
((Headline)) Railroad workers stop ghost train
((Lead)) Freight train rolled 80 km through Bavaria. The brakes had failed.

Those who rely on clickbaiting may have texted like this:

((Roof line)) Rolling time bomb
((Headline))Train speeds through Bavaria unchecked.
((Lead)) A freight train rolled through numerous stations at more than 100 kilometers.

However, it would also be conceivable

((Roof line)) Brake failure
((Headline)) Train rolls 80 km through Bavaria
((Lead/Teaser)) How railroad workers prevented a train wreck.

The different depth of information is characteristic for texts on the web. Many editors place a so-called "lead" or summary before longer articles: Here, the most important information is placed first – in any case, those Ws that you have selected as the most important for the first sentence.

In print media, the lead text "leads" the article – hence the name. Being able to write a lead text is part of the classic journalistic craft. If you want to know exactly how to do it, read "La Roche's Introduction to Practical Journalism".

What is meant by a teaser? The "teaser" or "teaser words" function on the home page as an introduction to the detailed article on a subsequent web page. In journalistic terms, they are similar to the first sentence of a longer article, which is intended to act as a "slide" into the article – with one significant difference: online, it is the teaser alone that determines whether the user even gets as far as the detailed article. Accordingly, a distinction can be made between *summary teasers, question teasers* and *announcement teasers* according to their content-related function (cf. the overview of teasers on the following pages).

The teaser almost always contains the headline, often supplemented by a line, sometimes also by the lead text. Sometimes it is only two to three words, in which the following content must be packed compressed. Teasers can be easily categorized by length: Anything from a two-word sentence to a headline/lead combination of more than 200 characters. Even if there is only a short sentence on the introductory page that is meant to entice you to read on, it is still called a teaser. It is then characterized by a length of usually less than 65 characters (= one long line or two to three short lines).

However, the teaser can definitely reach the length of a full-blown lead. Some news tickers on the web simply take the headline or the first sentence of the article as a teaser. This assumes that the article itself was written according to journalistic principles: The first sentence must contain the most important thing in Ws, the core message.

Quick overview is what the teasers are supposed to give the user. The news pages of practically all relevant media online prove this: Whether at Tagesschau.de or at "Spiegel", "Focus" or "Süddeutsche Zeitung" (South German Newspaper): The text in the news overview is short, factual and informative. The more in-depth information follows when you click on the teaser.

Recognition must be possible: Elements of the teaser should be repeated on the next, subsequent level: In the case of short teasers, the entire text, and in the case of multi-level teasers, the headline in any case. Therein lies the art of online preparation: Informing briefly and accurately, offering more in-depth information on the next level. The classic "principle of the inverted pyramid" also applies to the structure of news online: The new, the important, the special comes first, followed by the details. Only later come the details and the back story.

In this respect, the craft of news writing for online media hardly differs from that for the classic media. In addition to informative forms of presentation such as news and opinion such as commentary, there are even more forms available on-line – the following chapter "The interactive forms" is dedicated to them.

Teaser overview. Teasers can be classified simply according to their *length,* then according to their *function, and* finally also according to the journalistic *form of presentation* used.

The following types of teasers can be distinguished according to length and comprehensiveness:

Headline teaser that puts the information content in abbreviated form. In this form, the whole teaser acts as a hyperlink, example:
  Japan's economy is growing.
  Woman died of flu.
Headline plus text. In this form, not only is the heading marked as a hyperlink, but the text is extended by a symbol (such as an arrow) or an addition ('More ..., Continue, Read more ...') that links to the detailed document.
  "The world is against us"
  Both Israelis and Palestinians see themselves not as perpetrators but as victims. There can never be peace like this.

Teaser with image as lead: Longer teaser forms almost always contain an image. If they are the first text in an online offer, they perform the same function as the lead in a printed newspaper.

Speed limit debate

The SPD wants a speed limit on highways
But the plan has no support in the Union. One SPD politician calls Transportation Minister Scheuer's no a "petulant" statement. The FDP is also against a speed limit. **Imore**

Teaser with image as lead story at tagesschau.de, December 26, 2019

We distinguish according to their *function*:

Summary teasers
represent the information core of the following website:
'Craft trades expect sales to fall'.
    A question as a teaser requires repetition of the question and immediate answer in the following text:
'Corporate quiz: Do you know Germany's secret giants?'
'What do the stars say today?'
    Announcement teasers merely describe what follows:
'A city parties. Where to party, eat and stay best in Stockholm and lay on a beach in the middle of the city'.

But teasers can also be classified according to their *journalistic form:*

News teasers are a common form: They inform without expressing an opinion.
'Tax reform: relief for small and medium-sized enterprises'.
    Commenting teasers and teasers with an appealing character are often found online in addition to or instead of the headline. They are often combined with the invitation to participate in participative forms such as discussion forums of the user community.
'Lafontaine's Big Bluff'

Chancellor Angela Merkel **podcast** was anteceded in November 2019 as follows:

The German government wants to work with the automotive industry to drive forward the transformation of mobility. On Monday, the strategic dialogue will take place for the second time. In her latest video podcast, Chancellor Angela Merkel names three core areas for the meeting: the promotion of alternative drive systems, the expansion of the charging infrastructure and the impact on work in the automotive industry. The

future of mobility will be thought of in a much more networked way, the chancellor
said.
  https://www.bundeskanzlerin.de/bkin-de/mediathek/die-kanzlerin-direkt/
podcast-mobilitaet-1687758!mediathek?query =, December 26, 2019.

The teaser brings the central information. Even those who do not watch the
video are informed.

The principle of increasing depth of information is characteristic of hypertext. What is new compared to linear writing is the division into different documents: Headline and teaser provide the basic information. Online, the teaser is on
a different screen page than the subsequent text. Details follow after clicking on the
teaser. Here the information becomes broader, the information content less dense.
Parallel to the increasing depth of information, we speak of the *decreasing density
of information*.

Further links reinforce this principle: As a rule, they lead to the original
source of the information. This is usually not as well prepared as the online journalistic article. But it contains more details. In the example of the 66 Hamburgers,
one could link to the original statements of the artists. When deciding whether this
link is necessary and helpful, it is helpful to ask the question: Does the user get an
additional benefit from it? In the example, this question could be confidently answered with "No".

Net reportage and net dossier. Online-specific forms of presentation work ex-
tensively with the possibilities of associative and in-depth information links. The
net report provides the user with an overview of a current topic in the main text, for
example "Right-wing extremism on the Internet". Text links lead to the addressed,
mostly external sources; below the text, the links are again systematically listed
and often commented on. A network dossier, on the other hand, consists of several
separate contributions on a topic; it usually contains internal as well as external
links.:

How long can coherent texts be online? The derogatory term "chunk journalism" is often applied to online formats. By now it should have become clear: Long
texts are definitely allowed online – but they must be structured in a user-friendly
way, cf. the following article "Links structure the reading flow". Online media in
particular offer the possibility of letting the user decide on the desired depth of information. A link to further information may therefore refer to the 80-page scientific study on the topic if it is announced correctly – the user does not have to follow
it.

Offer print version and download. Quite a few users download long texts to
their own PC or mobile reader, save them there or print them out on their own

printer. In this case, it is particularly helpful to offer the user a print version. An option to download the complete 80-page study also helps users to keep their online time short and to select the desired depth of information offline at their leisure. For such documents, choose a standard file format such as PDF, which is compatible with all computer systems.

Citing sources underlines credibility. There is a persistent rumour that information from the Internet is considered *less credible* than printed information. It dates back to the early days of the Internet, when there was no talk of independent online journalism. It is true that online, for the user, reputable sources are superficially indistinguishable from dubious ones. However you assess your own online offering: If you want to create credibility, name sources, first of all your own address. According to German media law, you are obliged to have an imprint anyway, see the chapter on *law*. There you will also find legal information on the subject of "setting links".

Do not be afraid of redundancy: When the user sees the following text on the screen, the previous one is gone. Similar to radio journalism, the repetition of core statements is therefore not harmful, but helpful. In particular, core concepts need to be repeated. Otherwise, you leave the user puzzled: Am I still in the right place here? Hardly any user has such a trained memory that he still has the content of a page he just skimmed – and now clicked away – completely in his head.

Some common misconceptions about online speech we can dispel at this point. One is "write like you speak!". True, online speech has more in common with radio speech than with "writing as printed": Sentence structure is simpler, word order is clearer, sentences are shorter. However, this has nothing to do with everyday speech, its verbosity and grammatical liberties. In contrast to spoken language, online language is concise, clear and polished.

Closely related to this is the warning against repetition – a second common misconception. Radio texts require repetition, radio broadcasts a certain redundancy, because a listener does not have the entire text present after hearing it once. The same is true online, as has been shown: Because the online user does not have the entire hypertext sequence present, repetition of headline, of parts from lead and teaser help him to understand the page that is currently in front of him.

The third big misconception is that online language is advertising language. It comes about because online advertising offers dominate – far ahead of journalistic offers. The distinction works here just like in real life: In journalistic texts, the rules for journalistic language apply – in advertising texts, those for advertising language apply. And you should be clear about what you are writing.

Two online reading types can be distinguished: those who are looking for information quickly, also called "horizontal" readers. They need everything at a glance, on one level. Skimming the teaser is enough for them. On the other hand, there are the "vertical" readers, who enjoy taking in more in-depth information. If they invest even more time, they become surfing, browsing readers: They follow the continuative links to get information directly from the original source if possible.

Most online offers track or scan user behavior. Depending on the usage situation, the reading types change. All online readers put together their own individual menu from the wide range of a news site online.

When writing hypertext, those who work specifically with teasers, links and the principle of increasing information depth, both types of readers will be satisfied. At the same time, the claim that online every piece of information has to be broken down into small morsels is taken out of focus. Longer texts are possible online – if they are provided with a good teaser and a useful lead and are clearly structured with links.

Flat text hierarchies are manageable, loose networks invite reading. Small units are inevitable on the entry page – certainly. But browsing through longer documents that are not hierarchically but associatively connected can be particularly appealing and provide impulses for one's own associations and insights.

The fact that setting links is an art of its own, which this textbook deals with intensively, is already becoming apparent. So far, we have only worked with the site-internal link from the teaser to the text, as well as setting another link that leads either site-internally to an earlier article on the topic or externally to the original source. More on the topic of "Links structure the reading flow" can be found in a separate article on the following pages. However, please note already here: *Don't link too soon!* Otherwise your user will be gone.

4.2   Links Structure the Reading Flow

For a short informative article, the gradation teaser – text with its distribution on two levels is sufficient, possibly supplemented by an external link to the source. Links, however, are not only the joints that connect the parts of the text framework with each other, they also present the user with decisions in more extensive online texts: follow the link or not? Follow this link, or another? To put it dramatically: the user stands in front of a hypertext with links like Buridan's donkey in front of two haystacks. The donkey eventually starves to death because he cannot decide. Users, on the other hand, simply visit another site – and the online offer starves.

Good links help the user decide. As nice as it can be to be surprised: When searching for information, you do not always want to be faced with new surprises, but rather be able to assess as quickly as possible: Is it worth following this link or not?

Unreal hypertext forces a decision on the user. If you write a crime novel, you design it linearly, for a whole book: you should not read the ending before the middle section, otherwise the tension is gone. The closer a journalistic form approaches classical literary forms, the more linear it is.

A column or gloss cannot be read in any order: Thought leadership and linguistic wit are linear in structure. Such forms of presentation can, if at all, almost only be brought online as a complete text. It does not matter if the column is a bit longer: many users print it out and read it at breakfast or at their desk.

It is also possible to work with a forced corset of links that imposes linearity on the user, whether he likes it or not. The structure of such an online text with *enforced linearity* then looks like Fig. 4.1.

You will find them online whenever you need to get a certain message across for content, educational or marketing reasons. Classics of this form are image galleries, with the help of which a story is told. A trick are curiosity-raising teasers at the end of a page, so-called *cliff hangers,* known from conventional television, which are supposed to make clicking palatable to the user. Oddly enough, what works wonderfully in print or broadcast media usually does not work online. Instead, the forced sequence of events – no matter how exciting – generates growing resentment in the user the longer it takes.

Tunnel structure is what the marketing people call this sequence, which takes away the user's time and action autonomy: He must submit to the pre-planned time sequence. This can make sense with a photo story or a didactically structured self-learning offer: With almost any learning material, one learning step at a time must be done. When answering the test questions, the user is offered several possibilities, but only one is correct. The tunnel structure has little to do with hypertext, because the user is relieved of all decisions regarding the sequence.

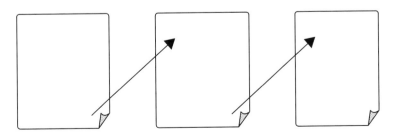

Fig. 4.1 Linear navigation

But the joke of online reading is the interactivity with its choices for the user. Links should be signposts – not puzzles, but help the user decide which direction to click on. Besides, they dissolve the notorious "lead deserts", remnants from the Gutenberg era, and structure even confusing amounts of text.

With service contributions this type of structuring can be observed particularly well. For example, medical portals such as onmeda.de structure their contributions according to the criteria overview – causes – symptoms – diagnosis – therapy – prevention – sources, cf. here using the example of back pain: https://www.onmeda.de/krankheiten/rueckenschmerzen.html (retrieved December 26, 2019).

In-page links that lead to so-called anchors or jump marks help to structure a long text. To do this, imagine the text as continuous, as if unrolling from a papyrus scroll. Only a section of the text fits on the screen. Because you do not know the technical equipment of your user (screen resolution), you cannot even say exactly how much of the text fits on his screen.

The only thing you know for sure is that the beginning is definitely visible.

The on-page text links take advantage of this. They were invented to make student seminar papers with their strict structure suitable for the screen.

The principle is simple: At the beginning of the text there is the abstract, followed by the table of contents. Each chapter heading leads to the corresponding chapter when clicked on, see graphic on the following page.

For longer texts, do not forget to always include links to *jump labels at* the top of the table of contents in between. This makes it easier for the user to keep track of the overall structure of the text.

Further links can round off such an article: to the page of the journal on which a study is described in detail, to a research project or to an overview page of another provider on which research results on social media are presented (for an independent online magazine).

In server terms, the last type of link described is also called an *external* link. The rule that such links should never be placed at the beginning of a text refers specifically to them. On the other hand, links that draw the user deeper into one's own text, into one's own offer, are expressly permitted at the beginning of a hypertext!

What types of links are there? Links can be distinguished in terms of *server technology, design technology* and *content.* The simplest distinction is the server-technical one, i.e. according to where the link leads to:

In terms of server technology, we distinguish between **three types of** hyperlinks:

- *on-page* links that lead to a jump target (anchor) within the present document,
- *site-internal* links, which remain within the online offer, but refer to a new document,
- *external* links that lead to another server.

The design decision in which window the target document is opened **also** has consequences for the reading flow.

In terms **of their content function,** there are completely different types of links. Some help to grasp the entire hypertext, others provide short additional information, others lead to longer documents. To find one's way around extensive online offers, entire link bars or columns are usually used, and even direct feedback can be regulated with a link.

We distinguish five functions:

- *Structuring* links divide the page. They have a comparable function to subheadings in a printed magazine;
- *Defining* links explain individual points in the text. Examples are references to a glossary or bibliography (example: Telekolleg Deutsch of the Bayerischer Rundfunk);
- *Associative* links lead to in-depth articles that are equivalent to the document just accessed. Example: Links to other articles of the same online magazine (example: http://www.zeit.de);
- *Navigation links* usually appear bundled together as a *navigation bar.* They help to select levels within a hypertext offer: within the same level, one level higher or lower;
- *Communication links* open a "New e-mail message" window or lead to further community services.

In **terms of appearance, all links are the same:** underlined and/or highlighted. The main problem for the user is that he does not know what type of link it is. This is a great way to mislead users. A widespread bad habit, for example, are personal names that are underlaid with links without explanation. The user has to try it out: If I click here, will I find out more about the person, their date of birth, their CV – or can I then send them an email?

It is true that the clever user informs himself in advance about the target of the link by simply pointing to the link with the mouse without clicking on it. It is fairer to inform the user by text or symbol what kind of link it is. Example: The easiest way to show that a communication link only leads to an e-mail address is to place a letter symbol next to the name.

But what if the visualization is not clear or a user prints the text? Then the information about the jump address is gone. The Internet journalist Martin Goldmann therefore recommends explicitly including e-mail addresses as well as web addresses in external links, for example:

'For more information, visit BMW at http://www.bmw.de.'

It is also helpful to specify the complete path or *deep link,* something like this:

'Find out more about online journalism training at http://www.Journalistenakademie.
de/index.php?p=3.'

Link texts must not be too long. A short headline of up to six words (rule of thumb – there are longer and shorter words …) is suitable, multi-line sentences or sentence fragments are not. In such cases, it is recommended to differentiate between headline and lead text and to use only the headline as a link.

Talking link texts. The user must know what he will get when he clicks. Each hyperlink must be labeled in such a way that the reader knows immediately whether there is information behind it that is of interest to him. Labels like 'Click here!' evoke the obvious question from the user: "Why should I?"

Multiple references to the same document are explicitly allowed! Hypertext consists of a network of documents, not linear processes. Avoid that your target document is only referred to from one navigation point, but on the contrary create several possibilities to get to the target document:

Buttons and text as links: A popular mistake is to make only graphical elements (buttons) clickable in a list with links and preceding graphical bullets. This confuses. When combining graphics, text, and links, place links after all elements, i.e., after the button and the text.

"Orphaned pages" and "dead links": Outdated web pages are usually either deleted or moved to the archive. If you do not do this, you end up with orphaned pages that currently no longer have a link pointing to them. Conversely, after some time you may have links on your site that lead to nirvana. Therefore, check all links – internal and external – regularly to make sure they still work. Special utilities or good content management systems check your links automatically.

The subsequent page must be understandable on its own. The user does not follow a predefined path. He can come to a web page either via the start page of an online offer, or via search engines and links of other websites. So you cannot assume, as you do with a book, that the reader knows the previous page. This is another reason why repetitions are necessary!

Links should be usable and reliable, *usability* and *reliability* are the requirements. What does this mean? The demand for usability of websites was set up by Jakob Nielsen. His website (http://www.useit.com) is a must for online journalists. "Amazing, but true. Jakob Nielsen's rules make sense even in times of higher bandwidth and new browser generations" judges online journalist Fiete Stegers. 2.

Jakob Nielsen's concept of usability linked technical criteria with content criteria and design rules. Nielsen's technically based rules from 1996 are no longer to be followed slavishly. However, Nielsen's warning against always using the latest technology cannot be emphasized clearly enough: Whether a web offer is aimed at technology freaks or young users, at senior citizens or people with disabilities: It is simply impossible to estimate whether *all* users of this target group 1. always have the latest hardware and software equipment installed, 2. are always able to install the latest software updates.

The online offer should always be usable with the older software version. Actually, online journalists should always design for the worst possible online equipment, and users should strive for the latest software. In fact, however, it is usually the other way around.

Nielsen warns web designers against flashing text and constantly running animations. The validity of this requirement is also undisputed and proven from perceptual psychology: Elements that are constantly in motion occupy a large part of human perception3. Too much of it distracts the visitor to a website. In addition, texts that run "off the reel" impose a time structure on the user, as with television – but users prefer to have control over time.

Nielsen's rules have lasting validity where they address linking and navigation: Every single web page must lead back to the start page, or at least one level higher. With a maximum of two mouse clicks, the user must be able to find out what this page belongs to and in what context it is located. This is usually taken care of by a well-designed CMS. Nielsen's sentence "Never assume that a user knows as much about your site as you do" can stand as a basic rule above the following contribution to the navigation structure of a website.

The Annenberg Journalism School has established the **requirement for *reliability* of links.** The term encompasses *reliability* as well as the aforementioned *predictability* and *traceability:* it must be apparent to the user in advance where the link leads, whether to an external offer or to a further text within the site, whether to a video or to something else entirely. But reliability also means: the link must not lead the user astray or in circles. It must be subsequently comprehensible why the link leads exactly here and not somewhere else.

Flow effect: If everything is right, the user will have the desired flow experience, as Thomas Wirth calls it (http://www.kommdesign.de): The user navigates through the hypertext as if by himself.

The term "flow" was coined by the American psychologist Mihalyi Czikzentmyhalyi in the mid-70s. He examined activities such as playing chess or mountain climbing – actions for which the corresponding knowledge and skills are necessary. Ideally, in flow, skill and result are in balance for the performer.

Mastering the task generates pleasure. If the task is too difficult, it is abandoned; if it is too easy, the user becomes bored. Thomas Wirth's conclusion: The more demanding the – mastered – task, the more intense the flow. Websites that achieve a flow effect with the user are gladly visited again.

4.3   Navigation for Mobile Touch and Voice Control

The majority of users receive online texts on mobile devices; more and more users use voice input devices. Here, too, rules have developed for ease of use.

Gesture control on touchscreens is largely standardized. There are

- Touch
- Wipe
- Pull
- Pull up or down.

Analogous to the desktop user interface, a back button, a forward button and a home button are offered. Since the display and thus the visible text section is small, the three factors language of the texts, size of the texts and structuring of the content are even more important here than on the desktop.

We pay attention to the size and contrast ratio between fonts, controls and graphics.

Menu bars are used for navigation and offer the appropriate selection options (navigation points). The so-called "hamburger navigation" is very common. The menu is hidden behind the icon with the three crossbars, the symbolic sandwich or hamburger. If you tap on it, it opens as a drop-down or as an *off-canvas* that slides over the page content from the left or right.

The canvas is the section of the screen that can be designed. If you scroll horizontally, i.e. move the "canvas", you can display content from the "off".

A *carousel* is another navigation option: Some navigation points are visible next to each other on the screen, others can be brought into view by swiping.

The opened menu item can be closed again in the same way. An off-canvas navigation from the left should be able to be closed either by swiping to the left or by touching the "X" symbol.

Users must be able to see whether a menu item leads directly to a page or to a further sub-level. Main categories and subcategories must be clearly distinguishable for them. If the menu items are not large enough, they are not easy to tap.

A distribution page can be structured well with tiles. Each image tile leads to a subpage. In the desktop navigation, the tiles can be seen in several rows and columns next to each other. On the mobile screen, they are arranged next to or below each other depending on their size.

Also typical for mobile devices with small screens is the "accordion" navigation, which works similarly to the navigation with jump labels described above: The desired content is unfolded by tapping on it, the remaining content remains visible only as bullet points.

In the case of voice input, the individual characteristics of the user must be taken into account to an even greater extent. The central consideration is the goal with which the individual person uses the interface. So that the short-term memory is not overtaxed, no more than three, maximum five points should be offered for selection. Concise and comprehensible feedback helps with voice navigation.

User scenarios such as the persona concept help to systematize the different usage situations. Such a persona is given a name, an age and possibly a short biography such as "Sandra, 45, lawyer in Hamburg" as well as a functional description: "is looking for the current decision of the Hamburg Parliament on the obligation to provide information".

4.4   Storyboard for the Navigation

The memorable image of navigating through the floods of information dates back to the early years of the Internet: Paul Gilster directly named his introduction to the then-new medium "Navigator." And after all, that was also the name of one of the oldest browsers: Netscape Navigator. The navigator image has three essential aspects: (1) the activity, the decisions of the helmsman based on his knowledge and experience; (2) the maps, the compass and other navigational aids at his disposal; (3) the duration of the journey – the temporal dimension.

The only question is: Who are the navigators? The journalists who steer their users, the passengers, safely through the dangerous flood of information? Or the users themselves, who take the steering wheel in their hands? What role do online journalists have if the classic *gatekeeper function* no longer exists?

In today's information worlds, everyone is their own navigator – that much is certain. Anyone who designs online worlds as a media maker must take these three dimensions into account: the actions and goals of their users, the site, the plan of the terrain ("site" literally means: location, terrain), and the timeline on which the navigating user's journey takes place.

Action, locality, duration – the three determine the *navigation,* the *site map* and the *storyboard* with its timeline. Storytelling online: How do you build a script, an engaging outline, meaningful navigation that supports *flow* for a multi-page, thematically related online product?

Using the example of a network dossier on the topic of "Mass Drug Alcohol", we show how an idea first becomes a collection of material, then an outline and finally a structure for an online dossier. From this, the channels, the navigation bar and finally the start page develop.

Who is the offer intended for? Not only because of the possible cooperation partners and advertisers, the question of the target group is central. Should young people be addressed, parents, teachers or even colleagues, i.e. media makers and multipliers? Do you want to inform the ignorant about a topic or give those affected a forum for exchange? The answer to these questions has a decisive impact on the content of the dossier – that is why it comes at the beginning.

Which strategy you use depends on your client. To stay with the seafarer's image, one wants to selectively filter out the flying fish from the ocean of users – the other thinks more of the trawl method. There are good reasons for both strategies – and excellent methods of market and media research to help you decide. Sometimes a good nose is said to bring amazing successes for seafarers and journalists alike.

In the example of "alcohol as a drug", young people come to mind as a target group, as well as parents, teachers, other educators and, in the business sector, alcohol among colleagues/employees. The trigger for your article, however, is the spectacular drunk driving of a well-known politician who is now threatened with the suspension of his driving licence. That is why you decide to focus on "Alcohol in the workplace".

Criteria you should consider when collecting:

- Who is the online offer intended for?
- What special benefit does the user get from your dossier?
- What content fits those people you want to target?
- How does the online dossier fit into your overall online offering?
- What feedback and communication options should it offer?

What is already available online, and how is your offering different?

Brainstorming is a good way to find ideas for the dossier. Together with your colleagues or alone, write down all the ideas that come to mind. Do not judge – do not let thoughts like "can't do" get in the way! Record each idea on a coloured card or sheet of paper. Afterwards you can arrange the cards on the wall or on a moderation board. This already creates a first structure. Take half an hour for this.

The ideas should not be discussed at first. Possible results of the brainstorming "Drug alcohol":

Utility cooking recipes/cocktails:

– alcohol-free
– with alcohol…

Utility contact/help:

– Who can I turn to as a person affected?
– Who helps relatives?
– Who does therapies?

Tips for work colleagues/boss
Cooperation partners: catering trade/associations, in order to bring inexpensive non-alcoholic beverages into the catering establishments.
Portrait of a former alcoholic
Interview with the partner/life companion of an alcoholic
Medical: how does alcohol

– short-term
– in the long run

Talking to a therapist: How do I recognize vulnerability?
How does withdrawal work?
Establish contact/possible cooperation partner: Alcoholics Anonymous or similar self-help group
Social background: alcohol as a recognised, legal drug
Statistics: What percentage of the population are alcoholics?
Turnover with alcohol? Countries/federal states with the highest alcohol consumption?
Cooperation partners: all producers of non-alcoholic beverages
Cooperation partners: Health insurance companies
Alcohol in Art and Literature …

In a second step, you and your colleagues **discuss and evaluate** the ideas. Gradually, a few particularly important points and topics crystallize. If there is still disagreement about the goals, allow each participant in the discussion to award two or three points for the key points that are most important to them. The idea with the most points wins, and you have the main topic of your online dossier.

The **fact that the actual research begins now,** that preliminary research can be useful beforehand – online as well as offline – that conversations must be held, appointments made, concepts and many texts written, all this is classic journalistic craft. But this chapter is not about that.

The **value of the online medium** lies in its interactivity and communicativeness. What does your online dossier offer that a press product or a radio broadcast cannot? If you have an answer to this question, you have found the core idea for your online dossier.

In our example, this could be the possibility for those directly or indirectly affected to contact each other and self-help and therapy facilities. Concrete tips – as far as they can be given in a general form – also make up a high utility value. Personal statements from those affected illustrate the topic. Only then comes background information such as statistics and medical facts.

The **core of a good online dossier** is the clear concept with a multi-level information hierarchy. Systematic planning and tight online editing prevent the concept from "going off the rails". If you want to play along: Try to filter out a clear outline from the ideas above (or your own) onto which you can distribute the ideas roughly evenly. The result does not have to be a scientific paper with subheadings 3.1.2.7.1 to 3.1.2.7.12, but from *the individual user's situation,* allow him or her to choose: What interests her or him most, what would she or he like to read first?

Example concept for the dossier "Alcohol at the workplace"

- Effect
- Therapy
- Prevent
- Discussion (community with user forums and chat)
- Contact with experts and the editorial team

The topics are distributed among the individual chapters as follows:
Effect
Interview with the partner/life companion of an alcoholic
Medical: how does alcohol

- short-term
- in the long run

Social background: alcohol as a recognised, legal drug
Statistics: What percentage of the population are alcoholics?
Turnover with alcohol? Countries/federal states with the highest alcohol consumption?
Cooperation partners: Health insurance companies
Alcohol in art and literature
Therapy
Portrait and curriculum vitae of a former alcoholic
How does withdrawal work?
Utility contact/help:

- Who can I turn to as a person affected?
- Who helps relatives?
- Who does therapies?

Tips for work colleagues/boss
Establish contact/possible cooperation partner: Alcoholics Anonymous or similar
self-help group
Prevent
Talking to a therapist: How do I recognize vulnerability?
Utility recipes:

 – without alcohol (the editors wisely decided to leave out the recipes with alcohol ...).

Cooperation partners: catering trade/associations, in order to bring inexpensive non-alcoholic beverages into the catering establishments.
Cooperation partners: all producers of non-alcoholic beverages
Discussion
Three discussion forums correspond to the three headings – they are cross-referenced
in each case
Contact
The sections offer this function directly – but they also refer to the contact page.

The order in which the five chapters and thus the channels are then selected is
at the discretion of the user.

The **storyboard or script** that emerges from these ideas should be visually
implemented. You can use any presentation technique that is available in your editorial department:

* A *flipchart is* sufficient for a sketch in the simplest case;
* a *pinboard* with coloured cards is more flexible if you want to show a change quickly;
* Suitable *software,* from simple presentation programs to complex design tools, also helps with visualization.

Two strategies for navigation can be distinguished:

* the strictly hierarchical and
* associative or peer-to-peer navigation.

A strictly hierarchical navigation structures the dossier like a scientific paper
(Fig. 4.2).
This is already the pain threshold for the user: As a rule, he cannot keep track of
more than three levels.

Peer-to-peer navigation basically sees all pages as equal, as can be seen in
Fig. 4.3.

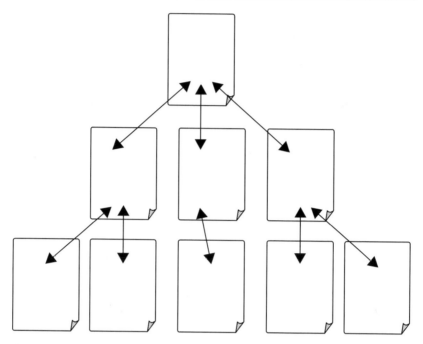

Fig. 4.2 Hierarchical navigation

The requirement that each page must be understandable on **its own** is obvious in this model: the communication effort (what does the user need to know about the layout of the entire dossier?) is extremely high. The peer-to-peer model imposes extensive requirements for leads and teasers on each page.

The storyboard, a combination of pages and arrows, illustrates the chosen navigation strategy. In practice, both strategies complement each other. An example is Fig. 4.4.

We have taken the liberty of **simplifying** things: to avoid confusion, we have only included the second level for the "Therapy" section, and the third level lacks the cross-references between them – please think of them.

So a possible reading flow could look like this: From the home page to the tips for work colleagues, notice there that preliminary information would be helpful, back to the therapy page, back to the effect, browse there and then to the discussion forum (general interested user). Another: From the homepage to "How do I recognize …?", from there to the chapter "Effect", via the statistics to the tips, from there to the discussion forum (user with the suspicion that a colleague is affected). Or …

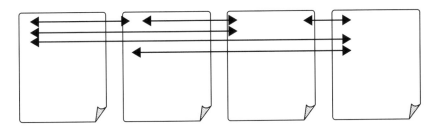

Fig. 4.3 Peer-to-peer navigation

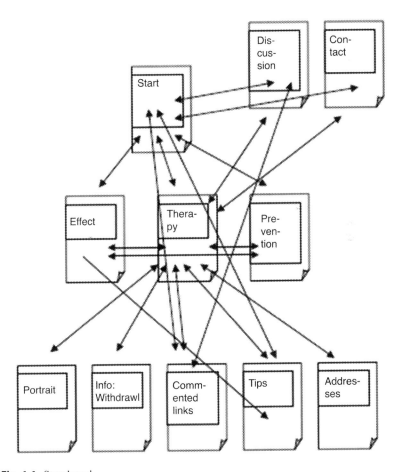

Fig. 4.4 Storyboard

the variations cannot all be listed. It must always be ensured that the user can reach a meaningful connection from any page.

Dramaturgy: Similar to a modern magazine layout, you can divide the content of your dossier into clearly arranged blocks. One possibility is to separate them according to the form of presentation: The interview gets a page as well as the info block, the commented links or the "net reportage" as well as the commentary. However you create your dossier: Make sure that the online journalistic forms of presentation are varied, as described in the following chapter. Loud reports strung together are just as boring as loud interviews or commentaries. In any case, you should ensure that you alternate between interactive and participative forms.

The rule of thumb "No more than three levels that the user has to keep track of, no more than four mouse clicks to a page" cannot always be implemented, but it works quite well as a guideline. The basic principle is that there is practically no page that links to only *one* other page – and no single page that is linked to only *from one* page.

Mandatory: Each page refers to the next higher level and to at least one other page. Within a level, related pages can be reached directly via navigation bar, the directly following one (in case someone reads linear after all) as well. From each page there are links to the discussion forums, to the contact page, to the imprint and to the start page of the entire online offer, within the framework of which the dossier is located.

In some cases text links (*hot words*) are recommended, especially for the pages of the same or lower level, in other cases generally understandable symbols (e-mail, homepage) are suitable. On the online pages for the book (http://www.online-journalismus.org) you will find examples of the design of such navigation aids.

Freestyle: Hypertext is ultimately non-hierarchical. Its charm is based on the fact that the pages with high utility value – such as the annotated links to institutions that can help a person concerned, or the tips for boss and work colleagues – can be referred to *directly from the front page of the dossier.* And of course also from the front page of the entire online magazine.

Consider user types: In our model above, the two models overlap: the strictly hierarchical and the loosely associative. There is a method to this: Users can be differentiated according to whether they proceed logically-deductively or more intuitively-associatively. You could also say: more controlled by the left or the right hemisphere of the brain. To ensure that each user type can cope with your dossier, you offer both navigation aids.

Designing for the users could be the motto above this entire post. What situation are the users currently in? They can choose the order in which they follow your hypertext – give them as good decision criteria as possible. For this you will need the tools *link, lead* and *teaser* on every page.

Visual aids are ideally provided by the editorial system or design software. These include a navigation bar with graphical elements (buttons) that displays all chapters of the same level on each page and contains the links to start and contact pages, as well as showing the subchapters of the pages directly below in the hierarchy. Additional text links encourage associative reading and *flow.*

First the outline, then the design. With the outline, you determine how you want to guide users through the site. Only when this is clear do you build a text prototype of your dossier. All links, all elements of a page should be pure, unformatted text – do without all design elements at this level, similar to the way theatre rehearsals are initially done without masks and costumes. Using so-called style templates, you can first make the outline – later the design can be set up and modified without any problems.

We found an argument for simplicity in an old programmer's adage: only when a program is running properly do you worry about the design of the user interface. If you build the interface first and then change the program or, in this case, the site structure, the entire graphic development effort may be wasted. Another advantage of the prototype: It forces you to concentrate on the content.

What should the buttons look like, what should the navigation bar look like? With complex online presences, this decision has usually already been made: online journalists no longer have much influence on it. Exception: If you have the possibility to completely design a site. Then you are responsible for the conceptual design.

Everything else is the task of graphic and web designers and belongs in a textbook *web design.*

4.5   Usability and UX

The term *usability* derives from usable: usable, usable, usable, and was originally used for the interface between man and machine. Translations into German are a bit unwieldy: *usability* or *usability* of products. In online journalism, it describes how well an online product can be used in a certain context to achieve certain goals.

The "user experience" complements usability. This refers to all effects that the use of a user interface has on a user before, during and after use. Accordingly, both terms are applied to the usability of input devices of all kinds, from mobile devices to 3-D environments and mixed reality products.

In the meantime, there are sophisticated computer-aided measurement methods. The Poynter Institute was already a leader in measuring the usability of newspaper pages. Its *eye tracking studies* (measurement of the user's eye movements) still shape measurement methods today.

For the analysis and implementation of user needs, methods such as *Contextual Inquiry* are used, whereby the focus is on the user's action strategies and the context of use, *modeled reality with* the help of persona concepts and scenarios, *storyboards, wireframes,* and the development of *use cases* and *user stories. Design thinking* offers another user-oriented approach. In the creative process, six phases are run through in a few days and a result is achieved: Understand, Observe, Point-of-view, Ideate (idea generation), Prototype and Test.

4.6   Planning the Site and Homepage

If you have made it this far, you know the forms and formats that hypertext offers, and you are capable of building the navigation for a complex hypertext offering. Nevertheless, before you seriously start designing an entire portal or e-zine, we recommend that you first read the following two chapters: "Forms of presentation" on the retrievable online forms of presentation in the classic modes of text, audio and video, and "Participative forms and formats" on the online forms of communication.

Because your site, just like the dossier, lives from a change of forms and formats, from a dramaturgy of content. An online offer that ignores the *communicative added value* of online offers will not be able to sustain itself in the long run. In any case, your conception must take *organisational questions* into account: What does the workflow in the editorial department look like?

The **extent to which the workflow** is **determined by the software used** is one of the criteria you use to select the right *editorial system* (cf. the Chapter "The medium"). Have the *basic design* created by a company that specializes in magazine design (not: web design in general!).

Marketing questions also need to be considered for journalistic formats such as an online news offering: What is the unique selling point, the USP (unique selling proposition) of my online offering? If there is a parent medium, be it a radio broadcast or a trade magazine: What is distinctive about the *brand of* this parent medium? What needs to be taken into account to avoid a competitive situation between the parent and online media? In any case, the online offering should be developed in close cooperation with the parent medium.

Without a parent medium, the concept is freer, but also more difficult. Where should the content for your online offering come from? What do you want to focus on? You will find some tips and hints in the chapters "The Medium" and "The Participative Forms".

The commercial prerequisites must be clarified before you start designing. The classic methods of market and media research help here. Market analysis, market observation and market forecasting are their tools. As with any new product to be launched on the market, the ABCUV method must be applied:

* General economic situation and development
* Sector development
* Opportunities of the product/service
* User orientation: service motives and utility/added value for the user
* Distribution channels and cooperation partners.

Idea and title. Printed or broadcast magazines go to great lengths to find the basic idea and title of the product. Look at the other media: What do they call their magazines, and how are these formats defined? You will quickly come across titles like Report, *Post, Star.* But this does not exhaust the range of possibilities.

What is the central metaphor of your online magazine? If you think of the three dimensions *action, locality, duration,* which determine *navigation, site map* and *storyboard,* the metaphor search is not difficult:

Those who focus on *action* may choose the journey or travel metaphor. In this case, the focus is on the invitation to tour, explore or conquer. Such offers invite to a journey of *discovery or exploration,* e.g. http://www.perlentaucher.de.

Locality-fed metaphors for online offerings provide their users with spaces, journalists for example with a *newsroom* (editorial office). Those who offer conference rooms, meeting places, playing fields online design spaces for the users. The *chat room* also has a place as a basic metaphor.

Narrative, music and film structures define *time sequences* – not for nothing is there talk of *story* telling online. Theatre, film, TV: their central metaphors are called "performance", "show", "broadcast" – and for that you need a script. Anyone who visits the Tagesschau online, for example, encounters a sophisticated navigation and dramaturgy; anyone who visits http://www.bigbrother.de finds a community attractive to young users with chat rooms, forums and stories told via hypertext, which can be selected in any order.

The title corresponds to the central metaphor. The following basic strategies are possible: a name that is as eloquent as possible, which then also becomes the domain address, or a new word creation that is not yet associated with any meaning. In between are the original word games, which are also memorable. Examples of the first group are *rundschau.de, wetter.de* or *christkindlesmarkt.de*. Examples of neologisms are *xing.de* or *telepolis.de*. A more or less original title is *donnerwetter.de* (for weather information).

Content – from where? Do you and your editorial team want to provide most of the content yourself? Is there a parent medium that supplies it? Which and how much content do you want to buy in?

What special communication service does your online magazine offer? That is the central question in terms of content. For a politics portal, for example, this could be the possibility of organizing online campaigns; for a finance portal, it could be expert tips and analyses. Armin Gellweiler, editor-in-chief of web.de, talks about a *product portfolio*, a service mix for users.

Whatever design you choose, however your corporate identity (CI) and corporate design (CD) are set: Choose them clearly and concisely. A *style guide,* also called a *style book, will* help you to do this (see chapter "The interactive forms"). First and foremost, the appearance must be oriented towards the content and the needs of the users. In online journalistic formats, do without multimedia gimmicks, meaningless graphic animations beforehand and upstream pages that only contain the logo of your online magazine. These only slow down the user's search for information.

Do not succumb to the fallacy that you have to hide information and communication services so that the user has fun searching. Nobody wants to take the time for this. Therefore, answer these questions in a way that is as easy to find as possible:

• What does your site offer?
• Who are you?
• What makes your online pages so unique?

The start page is your first and last chance. Provide the user immediately with the first information and links to your content – this is how the portals do it: Right at the entrance there are current short messages and the cross-references. Make sure that your entry page is clearly structured and do not overload it.

In **order to get order into your topic offer,** a strictly hierarchical principle, which reminds of the directory and file arrangement on the hard disk, is suitable: From a main page, the user can access a topic subpage (channel), which in turn contains subpages. In this way, topics can be grouped together. In this structure, the user moves from information to information further and further into the site. You should also reproduce this structure in the directories of your server. Each new section ends up in its own folder.

On all more complex sites, such a structure is useful, for example, if you want to put a lot of texts or a portal with several sections on the net. The start page needs links to all sub-pages of the next level. It is ideal if there are hyperlinks to the next level but one next to these links. This makes orientation easier. Yahoo and other web catalogues work according to this principle (Fig. 4.5).

A start page for corporate communication using the example of http:// www.siemens.de: It uses the same techniques as a journalistic offer, but already addresses different target groups directly.

Navigation elements must be clearly visible and always in the same place on each page. For frame-based sites, put the links in their own frame. If you are working without frames, place the navigation elements on the left or above each document.

Visually, you should separate signposts from content. Depending on your graphic taste and talent, a horizontal line, a color highlighting or a separate graphic is sufficient. The result is a navigation bar that the reader will recognize on every page.

If you need multiple links, you put two bars. One is at the top of the page, the other to the left of the document. The top bar contains the links that are identical on all pages, such as the link to the homepage, to a search function or to the feedback

Fig. 4.5 Siemens

page. On the left, there are cross-references to further documents or subsections of a site.

Design serves the user. Do not start a new design experiment on every page. Web design does not primarily serve the artistic satisfaction of the designer. The design is in the service of the good usability of an online journalistic site. This means: The web page does not overstrain the resources of the user (client) and the server, the user feels addressed and he quickly finds his way around.

Especially this last point is important: The reader must not be forced to search. Those who first need a minute to decipher and assign the content quickly disappear again.

To do this, you need to know as much as possible about your target group. A radio station, for example, would do well to design its programme overview online in such a way that it can also be used by visually impaired people via voice output. Whether *barrier-free web design* is a must for a site, however, depends not only on the target group, but also on the provider: whether the site belongs to a federal, state or local authority institution (http://www.barrierefreies-webdesign.de).

Thomas Wirth points to **perceptual schemata** and mentions

- the reflexive response of our attention to movements or intense colors,
- learned habits, such as the order of gaze from top left to bottom right, which is dictated by the reading direction of Western culture,
- Internet-specific habits such as quick, superficial cross-reading of Internet pages (scanning),
- individual habits such as clicking away from pop-up windows or even the technical default of certain browser settings for fonts and colors.

Wirth also concludes, "The simpler the structure of a page, the less information presented at one time, the more clearly it is articulated visually, the easier it is to direct and control (the user's. G. H.) attention."

Further Reading

1. Dietz Schwiesau/Josef Ohler (Hg.), Nachrichten – klassisch und multimedial (Journalistische Praxis), Wiesbaden: Springer 2016
2. Steve Krug: Don't make me think! Web Usability – das intuitive Web. Frechen: MITP-Verlags GmbH & Co. KG 2014
3. Jakob Nielsen, Raluca Budiu: Mobile usability. Frechen: MITP-Verlags GmbH & Co. KG 2013

4. Michael Richter, Markus Flückinger: Usability und UX kompakt. Berlin-Heidelberg: 4. Aufl. Springer Vieweg 2016
5. Thomas Wirth: Missing Links. Über gutes Webdesign. München: Hanser 2002

Presentation Forms and Multimodal Formats

5

Abstract

What are the typical online forms and formats? The chapter distinguishes between information-oriented, narrative, opinion-oriented and service-oriented.

Online journalism requires journalistic know-how. The Internet transports content from all media: text, image, audio, video. The journalistic forms and formats from press, radio and television are not only adopted one-to-one but are also changed and adapted to the online medium. "Multimedia" and "Crossmedia" are frequently used terms for this; in the last decade, "transmediality" has also been added. Since online is about the different modes of reception reading, listening, seeing, we speak of *multi-modal forms*.

Anyone who wants to **produce journalistic content for the Internet** needs media-specific journalistic skills. This starts with writing concise, clear language and ranges from audio recordings of interviews to video journalistic documentation. It includes knowledge of journalistic forms of presentation, from the news item, feature or glossary to the conception of a comprehensive hypertext offering that combines several forms of presentation.

The user interacts with the server while surfing through hypertext – this is why we speak of *interactive* forms designed by journalists. On the other hand, forms are considered *participatory* if at least two people exchange information via digital platforms, from chat via Twitter to community (see the following chapter "Participatory forms and formats").

This chapter describes **which of the presentation forms are used in online journalism and how**: the *informative*, the *commentary* and the *service forms*.

© Springer Fachmedien Wiesbaden GmbH, part of Springer Nature 2022
G. Hooffacker, *Online journalism*,
https://doi.org/10.1007/978-3-658-35731-3_5

Multi-modal work is part of the daily routine for online journalists: The online presence for the weekly magazine must be coordinated with the print edition, the radio station's website with the current programs. Cooperation and networking make synergy effects possible. The article *"Mediengerecht konzipieren"* describes how to design bi- and multi-media and how to use the technology for this. In the following articles, according to their importance in online journalism, individual forms are presented in more detail, such as the interview or the newsletter. How they can be implemented in a media-compatible manner is addressed in the respective form of presentation.

I do not understand **blogs or podcasts** as forms of presentation, but as digitally defined formats that can be filled with journalistic content.

5.1   Designing for the Media

The majority of online publications complement a parent medium of press, radio or television. This is where cross-media concepts have their roots: the journalists quickly realized that a simple 1:1 transfer to the Internet was not enough. They each developed media-specific online forms. Mobile end devices, Internet via mobile phone change the possibilities of use and thus also the conception for the medium.

Rationalisation plans have changed the editorial organisation: The central *newsdesk* is where all media products come together. This is where it is decided which information is played out on which channel. The technology allows journalistic articles and their components to be managed independently of the output medium. For example: texts can be output for the print version or the online presence or read aloud by a machine via voice output, radio programmes can be published both on-air and online, video podcasts can be broadcast and made available in the media library. Journalists work online for several media or platforms (multi-platform journalism).

This convergence of journalistic products requires journalists who can produce competently not only for one medium but for several: not only for the printed edition of the magazine but also for the online edition; to work not only for the radio or television broadcast or the respective station but also for the corresponding online presence.

The mother medium and online editorial team must have a common concept: Weekly magazines such as daily newspapers are supplemented online with live updated information; monthly magazines offer appointment calendars and up-to-date information online. Specialist books and teaching materials, as well as this book, are expanded and updated through a comprehensive web offering. The website must match the magazine, and readers of the printed magazine must be able to find the special features of the brand online.

Conversely, user-generated information from the online offering is transferred to the printed edition: the best pictures from the photo competition among the readers, the best texts from the community go to the newspaper's youth page.

"**Mobile first**" replaced the slogan "online first" some time ago. My favorite: **Social first**.

The printed version of print products is not provided 1:1 for free use. This does not make sense for commercial reasons alone, because the print version is usually to be sold. However, media-specific requirements also stand in the way of simple transfer. There are various options for online publication:

- offer online teasers for the articles, for the long version refer to the paid offer at the parent medium;
- offer selected contributions online in their entirety, point out further contributions in the mother medium;
- especially for trade journals: offer online abstracts of the contributions, for which detailed information refers to the print edition or an archive for which a fee is charged;
- set up a completely independent online offer with independent financing or
- offer the print edition as *PDF* or *e-paper*, radio and television contributions as a *podcast* for download, also for a fee.

Contribution-financed offers such as those of the public service media can be made available free of charge via the media libraries, insofar as the legal framework permits.

The dreaded "cannibalisation of the mother medium" does not usually occur when the online medium is conceived and conceived as an independent medium in its own right. Then it is also attractive for advertising customers. Editorial offices where the interaction between online and print editions works report that new subscribers are added online. Broadcasters reach groups of listeners and viewers who were already thought to be lost.

Mutual references strengthen user loyalty: from radio or television to the supplementary Internet offer, from online pages to the print product, from newspaper or magazine to special offers on the websites.

Especially in the service area, synergy effects arise here, which on the one hand bring additional benefits to the reader or viewer when he or she also looks at the online offer, and on the other hand to the online user, who can download the detailed article, even for a fee.

Print media offer services **online for a fee** that were previously reserved for the advertising department – from job exchanges to real estate ads to dating agencies.

Radio and the Internet complement each other well because online offers exactly the two elements that radio lacks: text and images. In addition to direct listener service (programme overview, information on current or upcoming programmes), a radio station's web pages provide information that users can read up on at any time when they need it:

- News
- Weather
- Traffic information.

Such information can be taken over automatically by the online editorial staff. However, they then do not offer the increasing depth of information desired by the user. The online newsroom can link such short information with further offers or compile extended information.

An independent online editorial team is necessary for programme-accompanying offers: the exhibition review by the cultural editorial team is supplemented online by a picture gallery. The consumer magazine on the radio refers to the online service database, the music programme to the online dossier on the band or music genre.

The audio offer can offer an **additional benefit** for the online user if it makes the essential passages and original sound clips from current programmes available online. The core message of the conversation with the politician not only conveys the message but also brings the mood across – the reproduction of the entire interview, on the other hand, provides no additional information compared to the text version.

A *webcam*, which allows the studio guest to be seen live, or the chat, which supplements the broadcast, are also useful online additions to the radio.

Where online audio contributions are offered, a symbol should indicate this. When selecting the data formats, make sure that the most important available formats are offered (Fig. 5.1)!

The Internet is also a powerful tool for **TV service or educational offers,** as well as for supplementing news broadcasts. The online newsroom provides an

Commemoration of tsunami victims
Flowers at the Bahn station
Prayers, speeches and the hope that the early warning systems will work in the future mark the commemoration 15 years after the tsunami in the Indian Ocean. *Bernd Musch-Borowska was at a small railroad station in Sri Lanka.* **More**

Where the tsunami raged
What the region looks like today
Ships in the city, flattened houses and a single mosque: The pictures of the tsunami disaster in Southeast Asia in 2004 went around the world. What does the region look like today? **Pictures**

German economy
There hasn't been this much uncertainty for a long time
After a difficult year, German companies are cautiously optimistic about 2020. A glimmer of hope, but no all-clear - that sums up the mood in many companies. By Wolfgang Landmesser. **More**

Fig. 5.1   http://www.tagesschau.de combines the news overview in text and image with the program accompaniment. The TV camera shows where video streams are waiting

overview of the current news and links to more detailed information on the home page. Where video contributions are offered, a symbol should indicate this.

The difference between a classic television programme and a video contribution for online use can be easily studied by looking at the public news services: The *Tagesschau* is designed differently from the "Tagesschau in 100 Sekunden" for the Internet. In addition, the Tagesschau editorial team produces media-specific offers for social media platforms such as Instagram or TikTok together.

Knowing **the particularities of the respective platforms** is a prerequisite for the specific offers. A glance at IT publications often helps. In 2019, the magazine T3N has compiled the current image format requirements of the most important social networks in an infographic. (https://t3n.de/news/wp-content/uploads/2019/12/social-media-bildgroessen-2020.jpg) (Fig. 5.2).

Television, radio and the Internet are in a complementary relationship in the fight for the favour of users. The ARD-ZDF online study shows that the amount of time spent by German citizens on media is increasing overall. The media suffer differently from the increase in online use: The biggest loser seems to be the press at present. However, against the backdrop of streaming platforms, the television

Fig. 5.2 The "Tagesschau in 100 s" offers the shortest news in moving image format

offering is also changing from linear television to a platform that can be used with a time delay.

What do online journalists who want to work in multi-media **need?** The times when pen and paper were enough are over. Minimum equipment could be:

• Smartphone with a good camera
• Apps to control focus and iris
• Microphone to plug in
• Holder for smartphone and microphone
• Accumulators/batteries, chargers; connecting cables, power cables
• Mobile Internet access.

The software for (mobile) processing and cutting is added. A notebook additionally does no harm. You can find tips and recommendations for the right equipment in relevant blogs, for example at Björn Staschen.

Cross-media research: Video reporters have gained radio and television experience during their training, and have learned journalistic writing and conception. They plan strategically: The fact that the Federal President is coming to the opening of the fair is known weeks before the date. This is a good place to prepare the recording in terms of light and sound. The flood disaster comes suddenly – the video journalist must be on site quickly and document it as comprehensively as possible. *Before* the outside appointment, the video reporter plans who he wants to talk to and what he wants to record, and what he needs to record. Because there is usually no second appointment.

The concept includes the following considerations

- What can I research in advance online or by telephone?
- Who can I talk to on site? Which admission permits do I need?
- Which details do I have to research on site?
- Which elements are suitable for audio or video conversion?
- Which forms of presentation do I use (report as text, interview as text, audio or video, picture gallery, service box…)?
- Which settings do I have to film to be able to tell the story with moving images?
- How else can I visualize the theme (geo-tagging, animated graphics, cartoon…)?

The five-shot rule comes from video journalism. The first shot shows detail and action, thus possibly attracting the attention of the viewer. The second shot shows "who" is acting. Only the third shot resolves the situation. Then one looks over the shoulder of the person acting – like an apprentice or a secret observer, so to speak. If, for example, you take a picture of a cook cutting onions, the first setting is a close-up of the onion being cut by the knife. The second shot shows the cook's face close up, the third is a full shot of the situation, and the fourth shot looks "over the cook's shoulder". The last setting can be freely selected, but care must be taken not to go over the axis of action and a so-called *axial jump must be avoided*. In the example described, the action axis consists of an imaginary line between the onion and the tip of the cook's nose. (Fig. 5.3).

A textbook for video journalism cannot replace this book. For radio and television journalism there are proven and current publications. Reading tips can be found at the end of this article.

Calmer visual language, higher narrative speed. The visual language should become slower. Refined details, fast rides and panning to 8 cm width – that should be futile labour of love. At the same time, the narrative tempo increases: the 2'30"-Maz (with three o-tones, three off-tones) looks slow and boring on mini-screens. More effective are a higher narrative tempo and higher density. The text also becomes more important.

Interview with Malte Burdekat on the topic of video journalism

Fig. 5.3 Malte Burdekat on video journalism (https://www.gelbe-reihe.de/online-journalismus/malte-burdekat/ or directly https://youtu.be/vAb_cjnC4F4)

Mobile journalism requires specific approaches. While technology is becoming cheaper and lighter, the demands on journalists are increasing. Björn Staschen from Norddeutscher Rundfunk gives the following five tips:

1. History counts.
2. Switch the phone to flight mode before turning it.
3. Tidy up memory so that enough memory is available.
4. Clean the lens.
5. Let the phone guide you to find exciting camera angles. (http://www.gelbe-reihe. de/mobiler-journalismus/online-plus/)

Audio and video sequences are used when the same information cannot be conveyed equally well with text and photos. Messages do not necessarily have to be presented by a speaker; they can be recorded better and faster as text. The eye-witness of the accident, on the other hand, can illustrate his experience on video.

With audio and video recordings, as everywhere else, copyrights, as well as the rights of personality protection, must be observed. In principle, the consent of the recorded person is required, with restrictions for public events. Children may only be recorded with the consent of their parents. For more information, see the chapter on law.

Audio podcasts and audio platforms online are used intensively, especially when they don't cost anything. They save broadcasters the costly service of offering recordings of broadcasts on data carriers. The extent to which listeners are willing to pay a small fee for such a service is still to be tested.

Provide additional information value. The most exciting excerpt from Bill Clinton's speech before the investigating committee in the matter of Monica Lewinsky was viewed online by many users at the time, but the entire statement was not. Here it was the special additional benefit that the Internet offers: How Clinton averts his gaze, how he touches his nose, that is only inadequately conveyed by text and photo.

Offer communication benefits. The real strength of the online offer compared to television lies in its communication-oriented forms: News broadcasts are accompanied by discussion forums in which viewers can discuss current political developments. In cooperation with the online editorial team, entertainment programmes are developing new formats in which users can play the quiz questions. User contributions and requests are incorporated into the programme and have an impact on the further course of the game or plot. More on this in the chapter "Participatory forms".

Database in the background: no longer having information compiled and processed by people, but by programs – how is that supposed to work? People are still thinking: they determine how the data has to be arranged and recorded so that the user can select it according to his individual requirements and retrieve it on his end device, and they specify the steps.

"Editor algorithm": The compilation itself is done by programs that convert the steps into instructions (algorithms) The current news overview on news.google. de can serve as an example: It is generated fully automatically by the software. Further *news aggregators* have been added in the meantime.

Journalistic thinking is required to plan the actions of the users and to prepare the information accordingly. While online journalists have been dealing with user software up to now, from now on at least an understanding of standardizable information processing processes, that is, database programs is required.

Offer archive. Wherever it is possible in terms of licensing, broadcasters offer special programmes online for viewing and downloading. It must be possible to *search* for programme offerings *by topic*. A keyword search is recommended. The well-sorted editorial archive is also the basis for the development of media-independent journalistic products.

Anyone who wants to make an **archive available to his users** needs an appropriate *content management system* that provides a *database*. Databases consist of *data records* (example: details of a product), which are divided into *data fields* (examples: name, article number, description, photo, price). When designing the system, it is particularly important to ensure that all query options are considered:

What should the user be able to search for? Which search criteria should it be possible to link? Is full-text search necessary, and if so, in which field? The data fields are linked (relational and object-oriented databases).

XML (Extensible Markup Language) is closely linked to content management. Two main areas of application characterize XML. Firstly, XML is intended to simplify the exchange of data between programs. The developers were mainly thinking of databases and scenarios with distributed resources. For example, an online editorial department can use XML to forward database queries directly to a content supplier. Conversely, the editorial site requests information directly from the content supplier and merges data from different sources into a consistent looking collection. For the user, it looks as if the data comes from the in-house database of the online editorial office.

On the other hand, XML allows documents to be formatted differently depending on the medium. For example, a report can be written in XML and then prepared with simple instructions for publication via the World Wide Web or in the daily newspaper.

XML is not a separate page description language, but a tool for designing your own language elements and languages, each adapted to a specific purpose. With XML you are no longer bound to a given set of commands ("tags") as in HTML. The programmer defines arbitrary own tags. If required, he can also provide additional information, for example about the appearance or the data structure.

A clear separation into data (content), structure (of the data) and layout (presentation) allows much more flexible handling of information. Because regardless of the target medium, only the pure information, the content, can be recorded. And the information remains in its raw form. Other tools such as *XSL (Extensible Stylesheets) are* responsible for preparing the information. Information once captured in XML can be prepared for printing, web pages, mobile phone displays or even Braille devices that display Braille.

XHTML is an application of XML. If you know HTML, you can be happy: the familiar commands are retained. A 'table' works just as well in XHTML as in HTML. The main difference is that every XHTML document accesses a definition file. This file, called *Document Type Definition* (DTD), contains specifications for the data structure and syntax of the document. The browser uses a DTD to determine whether a document complies with these specifications and whether it can be processed further without problems.

Feeds, whether Atom or RSS, can be translated and interpreted differently. I like best the translation by Matthias Spielkamp to "real simple syndication" (RSS), namely "really simple distribution". Since XML is used to structure the data but independent of the layout, they can be made available as so-called feeds, headlines or teasers, in the form of "dynamic bookmarks". Users simply subscribe to the feed, which is automatically updated. If the user feels addressed by the teaser, he clicks on the full offer.

Feeds can be subscribed to. This distinguishes them from simply providing audiovisual contributions online. A podcast, whether audio or video, necessarily includes the feed that informs users about further episodes.

For the person who compiles pages for the web, it is worthwhile to deal with XHTML: One day you will understand better what the in-house editorial systems are doing. On the other hand, you can fall back on your knowledge of HTML if you are willing to learn a little bit more.

Metadata for content management. For the internal data management of individual *assets* as well as for cooperation with agencies or other external content suppliers, a precise definition of interfaces and data transfer is essential. Conversely, your own online editorial team acts as a content supplier for other media. In both cases, *metadata* helps with content management: structural information, so-called metadata, is collected separately for each file to facilitate exchange and archiving. This includes information about the *author*, the *topic*, the *time* and the *source* of the news.

International standards. The International Press Telecommunications Council (IPTC) sets worldwide standards in this area. To define the structure and content of multimedia data, the IPTC has created the NewsML standard, which is based on XML and is also called "XML for news". For text documents, there is the News Industry Text Format (NITF). It is used by Associated Press (AP) as well as by Dow Jones, the New York Times or the Deutsche Presse-Agentur (dpa).

NITF answers the questions:

- *Who* owns the copyright?
- *What* are the topics or events?
- *When* was this reported?
- *Where* was the news published?
- *Why does* it have a news value?

Heading, subheading or paragraphs are defined using NITF. To capture the subject, the *IPTC Subject Codes* were defined. This allows NITF documents to be searched faster and more targeted. More about this on http://www.iptc.org.

5.2   Inform: News, Slideshow, Interview, Podcast

That journalists should separate between information and opinion is one of the basic principles that journalism in Germany after 1945 has taken over from its US-American model. Before that, during the Nazi era with its press censorship and controlled media, the journalistic rule of separation had been suspended.

However, it has never been observed one hundred percent in Federal Republic journalism: Boulevard and entertainment formats allowed mixed forms from the beginning – across all media. Later on, *New Journalism* created independent forms through *storytelling*. Quite apart from the problem that objectivity in news journalism is the noble goal, but for various reasons is practically impossible to achieve.

Nevertheless, the journalistic principle of separation remains undisputed: It must be transparent for the reader where he or she is informed and can rely on the greatest possible factual accuracy – and where the journalist expresses opinions.

Message structure. The author of the following text has taken great care with the information:

> On Thursday, April 8, 2020, the annual general meeting of MediaForFun AG took place in Munich. As every year, the event started with a multimedia presentation of the CEO Maximilian Meier …

The user who reads this text to the end still has to be found. Why should he have to deal with something that obviously happens in exactly the same way every year? *News is news,* and the American journalist John B. Bogart's principle applies to this: "When a dog bites a man, that's not news, but when a man bites a dog, that's news". The man-bites-dog formula is over a hundred years old. Applied to the annual general meeting of the (invented) MediaForFun AG, it reads like this:

> The listed company MediaForFun AG is distributing around three million euros to its shareholders for the 2019 financial year. This is more than 30 percent more than in the previous year. The dividend rate remains unchanged at 21 percent; the total distribution amount increases because the share capital was increased to EUR 8.4 million from company funds. This was resolved by the Annual General Meeting on Thursday, April 8, 2020, in Munich.

The teaser also focuses on information. Many news sites adopt the first sentence of a post as the teaser. This assumes that this sentence contains the most important Ws, the core statement. How to find out what is the most important has already been described in the chapter "Hypertext" – therefore here is only a condensed summary. How to distribute the information between teaser, headline and text? On the start page, a teaser consists of a headline and short text:

MediaForFun: 30 percent more
The listed company MediaForFun AG is distributing around three million euros to its shareholders this year. More ...

If the structure of the message is correct, the most important information is in the first sentence (lead sentence). It is then usually also suitable as a summarizing teaser. If the user clicks on the hot word 'More ...', he will find the complete text including the headline on the next page:

MediaForFun: 30 percent more
The listed company MediaForFun AG is distributing around three million euros to its shareholders for the 2019 financial year. This is more than 30 percent more than in the previous year (etc.)

Further links provide the user, if he so wishes, with the detailed annual results, the balance sheet, the share price development of the last few years and background information on the company. The description of the links must make it clear who further information comes from the journalist? Or from the company MediaForFun itself?

Even if CEO Maximilian Meier should complain that the text is not coloured positively enough: it is informative and contains exactly what users of an online stock exchange service or the company's website want to know, who may hold shares in MediaForFun AG or be considering acquiring them: facts, facts, facts.

The chairman of the board would have liked it much better if the short article had been like this:

The Annual General Meeting of MediaForFun AG ended on Thursday in Munich with a super result after a mega-event for more than a thousand happy shareholders ...

For the user, it must be recognizable where facts are presented and where opinions are expressed: *Reporting, not judging* is the journalist's job. 'Super-Ergebnis', 'Mega-Event', 'happy Aktionäre': These are expressions of opinion – not information. The so-called *informational* journalistic forms of presentation such as news or reports do not contain any commentary by the author. In the example, facts are scarce – nobody will click further here.

The fact that even news is never "objective" has other causes: the selection, the order, the accompanying pictures … It is something else to put the expression of opinion into someone's mouth:

> "A mega-event", Steffi Brav is pleased. The 51-year-old table tennis player was a star guest at the annual general meeting of MediaForFun AG, which presented its annual results last Thursday in Munich …

The eighth W: "Who am I writing for?" changes the selection of facts. This text is too entertaining for the stock market report. However, it is o.k. for a magazine article in the "People" section of the (also invented) business magazine "Steffi", which is aimed at working women. Comment or not? No, because it *reports* on an expression of opinion; it is reproduced, clearly marked as a quotation.

Use opening credits or lead. The characteristic of informative texts on the Web is the different depth of information, as shown in the previous chapter. Place the *lead* before longer reports: In three lines or up to 200 characters, the most important information is at the top of the opening page – in other words, the Ws. The *report* on a separate page then becomes more detailed. Informative texts can be differentiated according to a length:

> **Message.** The shortest of the informative forms of presentation. It actually consists only of the journalistic Ws – and often not even all seven. Typical messages: Short news items (stock market reports, event announcements).
>
> **Message.** Like the message, but with a short explanation, further details or the history in one sentence. Length up to about 1000 characters.
>
> **Report.** Longer and more detailed (over 1000 characters). Can go into detail after the current results have been described, give a brief history and a preview of the next steps (e.g. in case of a legal dispute): "The chairman of the board announced that …". In further links, the user can read the history in detail.

Images support the information. Sometimes a photo is used online to tell more quickly than words about a well-known person, location or time – provided the person is visually present. Who would you recognize immediately from a photo: Michael Jackson – Ursula von der Leyen – Pablo Picasso – Marilyn Monroe – Steffi Graf – Josef Ratzinger? With whom would a symbol or an explanatory word be more meaningful?

Slideshows, often with an audio track, are an inexpensive alternative to more elaborate video contributions. Image processing programs or special software products help with the production.

Symbols for places, works and facts are rather a matter of luck: The fact that the Eiffel Tower stands for Paris, the Rialto Bridge for Venice, is probably well known, even the Brandenburg Gate for Berlin may still work. A violin for Stradivari, an apple for William Tell – that's where things get more difficult. In such cases, the following applies: the right word says more than a thousand pictures.

Multimedia and information: Amateur video of violent clashes in Berlin, the German Chancellor's New Year's speech in the original sound – please ask yourself critically: Is the information content of the audio or video document really so much higher than that of the text including the picture? Is a meaningful excerpt as an audio or video clip perhaps sufficient in addition to the text? Is the service for the user not greater if you select the decisive 30 seconds and make the entire video available for download on request?

The same applies to the annual shareholders' meeting or the entire press conference as video. You can offer a service with a short version that bundles the central statements.

Can information be entertaining? A magazine article, an interview, a report or a feature illustrates what news or a report means in factual terms. The entertainment value does not lie in the artistic presentation by the notorious "noble pen", the vain, self-indulgent journalists. With words, quotes or pictures, the report or feature gives the sensual impression of having been there. For all the joy of experiencing details as if you were right in the middle of it, the main value is still in the information that is conveyed. But something is different. How can this be grasped?

Personal coloration can be used as a criterion. Nevertheless, even a briskly written magazine article or video report is not an expression of opinion. The focus is not on what the online journalists think, but on what is described: the atmosphere at the annual general meeting, the facial expressions of the politician, the originality and spontaneity of the singer being interviewed.

Interpretation help is given – but nothing is "thought into" it. The journalists reproduce what they perceive and have recorded: the view of a detail, atmosphere, a fragment of a sentence that one visitor to the festival says to another. The users get the impression of having been there.

Instead of a description: the photo or the picture gallery. The destruction caused by the bomb explosion, the birth of the quintuplets, the wedding of the film actor: here the picture says more than a thousand words. "No page without a picture" can be taken as a rule of thumb even for longer informative forms online. Pictures sent in by users offer a popular opportunity for user participation.

Portraits of people are more suitable than group photos, and clearly recognizable objects are more suitable than photos that pose puzzles for the viewer.

An online women's magazine has tapped the photo gallery about the new autumn fashion on the homepage without a picture:

Wrap skirts, crumpled tulle and silk drapes with untrimmed edges – the new romantic look dispenses with sweet flourishes. Result: pure femininity

If you click on this summarizing teaser, you will get to the first photo, above which the following text is written:

The new romantic look dispenses with sweet squiggles. The result: silk drapes with untrimmed edges, crumpled pleated tulle and flower appliqués that step out of line. (http://www.elle.de)

The fashion journalist took a close look and described the fabrics and their processing. Her text for the first picture, which is followed by half a dozen others, merely repeats part of the teaser. Even if one can smile at the involuntary comedy of the flower applications that dance out of line: The online journalistic realization is a success in terms of structure.

The online journalist describes sensory impressions when photo or video is not enough: What does the visitor see, hear, smell when he accompanies the politician on her election campaign tour into the beer tent? When he has witnessed the pouring rain at the open-air performance of the opera? When he visits the Chicken Farm affected by the food scandal and talks to its employees? The journalist selects the impressions he describes according to how significant they are for the event.

The online magazine e-politik.de began its correspondent's report on the police riots at the G8 summit in Genoa in July 2001 **with a photo of the school stormed and destroyed by the police.** Despite the term "report", this form helps the user to evaluate and classify information from foreign regions. And this was the teaser:

'G8 summit in Genoa: so peaceful, so violent'

The reportage itself starts with two very different observations and elaborates on the subject by interweaving both perspectives – of the demonstrators and the police. The statements of the persons quoted are each backed up with figures.

Comprehensive research is the secret of these forms of representation. It is supplemented by counter-research: Is what the politicians, experts and press spokespersons say true? The web is well suited to finding out the telephone numbers or e-mail addresses of the interlocutors and informants, which are needed for reports, features and interviews, also for checking names, facts and figures. But then archive research and personal communication must follow. Data and names from the web are merely the basis for contacts, conversations, journalistic inquiries, interviews.

Facing **your conversation partner,** not online but *face to face* is still the best solution. A telephone conversation, a video conference via a screen, a chat in private or other forms of instant messaging can be accepted as an alternative solution. Their advantage is not only the convenient availability but also the possibility of recording, their disadvantage the extensive absence of what is covered by *nonverbal communication.* A wink of the eye, a telltale gesture, nervousness – all of these things come across worse or in a controlled (for professionals) way through electronic media.

Written questions by e-mail, which are also answered in writing by the interviewer, have one disadvantage: online journalists cannot immediately follow up on them. They may be sufficient for querying biographical data or simple statements – in any case, the spontaneity of direct conversation is missing.

Often an event or information is presented in a completely different way **at the scene of the event** than what is officially described: An old building district is to be renovated. The city administration presented its redevelopment concept with a lot of press coverage: Green zones are to be created, the houses gutted, the streets calmed down. Subsidies are available for the installation of modern heating systems and modernization of the old building stock. The online journalists have gathered this information from press releases published on the city hall pages of the city and from interviews with the parties in the city council and the building officer.

The counter-research here is the on-site research: the online journalist talks to the citizens who now still live in this district and finds out about the situation: After the redevelopment, rents will be more expensive. During the renovation work, many tenants will have to move out of their apartments. It is not certain that they will be able to move back into their old flats afterwards, because the flats will be partly merged and the division will be completely different afterwards. He notes the opinions of the residents, also looks at the area and several apartments.

Two objectives can be distinguished when conducting interviews: One is the *research* interview, which online journalists conduct with an interview partner to obtain information. The interview focuses on the interviewer and his or her statements. The journalist is often not seen or heard.

One only speaks of a journalistically conducted and prepared interview if the interview is also to be *reproduced as such* (publication objective): by text, audio or video.

According to Walther von La Roche, we distinguish three types of interview:

- to the point,
- to the person,
- to the opinion.

In practice, mixed forms often occur.

In any case, **the interview will be post-edited**. If you render it as text, shorten it to core statements and leave out repetitions, Uhs and Hms. Carefully adapt your interviewer's grammar to the applicable rules – you don't want to expose him or her. Regional peculiarities may be mentioned.

With the smartphone or video camera, you record what you watch for online offers. In other cases the digital audio recording device or notebook, organizer, or simply pen and paper are sufficient. In any case, observations, statements, quotations must be recorded immediately. You should at least note down the text for the web pages in keywords. Looking through multimedia material afterwards and extracting text from it is a time-consuming and laborious activity. In the case of audio and video material, you should record which setting shows what, and what is suitable for the online contribution. Remember every minute of recording: you must review, select and edit all the material afterwards!

> **Think about playback already during recording.** When you're recording, don't rely on the fact that you can cut and shorten everything afterwards. Conduct the interview in such a way that it can be published in an abbreviated form if necessary. Choose a setting that shows the interviewee in close-up – not the interviewer. If possible, work with two cameras to achieve more elegant cuts. Make sure that you have enough fitting cut images!

With professionals who are being interviewed, it easily happens to beginners that the interviewer takes over the lead. The result is pre-punched answers, just like those found in the company's glossy brochure or the party programme. That is why preparation is half the battle. You don't get information by smiling nicely at the interviewee and hoping that he or she will already tell you what to ask.

Part of the preparation is to find out at least the name and function of the interlocutor in advance as well as his basic opinion, his position on the topic. Details which one could not find out otherwise may be asked in advance of the actual conversation. Caution: Don't talk through all the questions before the actual interview – then not only the spontaneity is missing afterwards, but perhaps also some essential information.

The questions are written down on cards or pieces of paper so that the online journalist does not always have to consult his notebook during the conversation – this inhibits conversation. If the online journalist's questions are recorded via audio or video, the mnemonic device should be invisible in any case. In the conversation you can thus deviate slightly from the order you thought about before, prefer a question if it arises from the conversation, or skip it if it has already been answered. In addition, the answers are noted down on the respective piece of paper. That way nothing can get mixed up.

Questioning techniques can be learned. *Open-ended questions give* the interviewee room to answer; they are a good way to start a conversation. They start with 'Who?', 'What?', 'When?', 'Where?', 'Where to?', 'For what?', 'How?', 'How much?', 'Why?', 'Why?' or 'Why?' The person you are talking to can talk easily. *Closed questions* can only be answered with 'Yes' or 'No.' You nail the interviewer to a statement: 'Will you vote in the city council for the construction of the youth centre?' No interview can consist only of open or only closed questions. You have to decide on the mix.

Is it **worthwhile** to replay **the complete interview in the original sound online**? Isn't it enough to cut out the one or two core statements of the politician? For those who want to hear the complete interview, please make it available for download – please indicate the amount of data involved. Perhaps you will find out on looking through your material that a photo series of half a dozen pictures is enough to convey the atmosphere of the interview – then you'd better do without the multimedia overkill.

Checklist for the interview
Bring it:

- Prepared questions, material, contact details
- Smartphone or other recording devices, microphone, tripod (rechargeable batteries charged? Batteries, spare batteries? data medium/replacement?)
- In any case additional notepad and pen or electronic notepad

Detain on site:

- Personal data such as name, age, job title, title
- Address, local conditions
- Casual remarks
- Details
- Colours
- Moods.

Typical online interviews can be found, for example, with YouTuber Tilo Jung with his format "Young and naive". An interview format that already works in a completely participatory manner and does not require a journalist is "Ask me anything" (AMA) on Reddit (http://www.reddit.com/r/AMA/).

Live forms such as audio or video sent via livestream require more preparation, on the one hand, experience and spontaneity on the other. And a very good online connection.

Story formats on social media platforms are an **alternative.** Originally created at Snapchat, they have long been available on Instagram and other platforms.

Planning and conception are similar to those of a classic on-site-reportage. Since they require a community, more about this in the participatory forms.

News tickers and live blogs quickly create a chronological sequence in which the audience finds the current status at the top. At the same time, an archive of events is created. An example of the G20 summit in Hamburg 2017 can be found online at Die Zeit (http://www.zeit.de/politik/2017-07/g20-gipfel-hamburg-live).

Conversation. Several discussion partners discuss a topic. The online journalists are equal participants in the conversation; they control the course of the discussion. A conversational tone is permissible; the discussion partners are given more time (and space) than in an interview. A subsequent chat allows the user to communicate with the discussion participants.

To plan **a podcast,** first, define the target group again. Is there already an audience that can be addressed online, via social media?

Conversations are a popular podcast format. But with whom should the conversations in the individual episodes be held, and about what? Which moderation should it be – one person or two (double moderation)? In which role is the moderator on the road – objective, curious, representing the audience? Or would you prefer a flippant, punning manner? Advisory or commenting? Where should the podcast appear, and how often, with what frequency? Which elements should appear in each individual podcast episode, which are variable?

Plan at least the first three podcast episodes with interview partners and an approximate discussion sequence in key points. Do not read the questions – you can hear that. A good interview guide anticipates possible developments in the interview and leaves room for unexpected developments. You should plan the end as well as the beginning.

Write a synopsis,
in which you answer the most important questions for your podcast:

* When and in which frequency should the podcast appear? On which platform?
* Are one or two people moderating?
* What kind of facilitation role are you planning?
* What regular elements should the individual sequence contain?
* What are the scripts for the first three episodes?

For the technical implementation, you need at least one good microphone and ideally a booth suitable for speakers. An overview of free software for audio editing can be found online.

5.3   Narrative Formats: Onepager, Newsgame, Web Reportage, Web Documentary

Web reportage and web documentary inform from all sides, not only from one line of sight. Online they combine forms of presentation such as audio or video reports with texts, picture galleries, game and VR elements. They thus represent collective formats that combine several individual contributions into a whole.

Web reportage or web documentary replaces online the classic text reportage as known from newspapers and magazines. But similar to the reportage, observations of details illustrate the facts and figures of the situation. The reportage start page contains an overview of the individual articles. Important are quotations and personal statements of affected persons on all pages. Contradictory statements are contrasted with each other. Figures should be visualised in charts and diagrams, chronologies should be presented as text, experiences during research as text, audio or video, and links to further information should be placed at the end of the report.

Photo slideshows are a good idea for travel reports, for example about the palazzi of Venice. The magazine Geo offers a whole podcast series. In an audio report as a podcast episode, the then head of the Geo online editorial department Jens Rehländer already described his experiences on a trip to the lagoon city with his family in 2009. Readers also have their say in travel blogs.

Animated (moving) single images and graphics have become more and more important online. For travel reports, the 360-degree panoramic view is often the best option. Edited and animated photographs and diagrams serve to illustrate technical or scientific contexts.

Image series regularly achieve high click rates. They often complement reports or network dossiers (see below). They can be presented either as a picture gallery, which gives the user an overview in the form of thumbnails before he can enlarge individual photos with a click. A linear form of presentation, in which the sequence of the images is determined from the outset, is also common.

Web reports usually combine text, audio and video elements on one extensive page. They are therefore called Longread or Onepager. Occasionally one reads the name "Snowfall" after a famous example from the New York Times, the avalanche accident at Tunnel Creek (http://www.nytimes.com/projects/2012/snow-fall). Because of its size, it is also called *scrollytelling*.

The users decide in which order they receive which elements (and which not). Web reports are usually implemented with special software. Pageflow" is widespread among public broadcasters. This quarks report at WDR takes the audience to the last orangutans (http://reportage.wdr.de/quarks-sumatra-webreportage).

Blogs also use this form, for example for travel reports. The web report can contain numerous text links. The user is told what he will find when he clicks on the specified sites. The links are usually put together again at the end of the web report.

Portraits can be structured similarly to reports **online**. A personality is introduced, biography and meaning are sketched out, spread over several documents. Media changes can be incorporated online: Photo, short video, sound bites, text information. Historical persons can be brought to life through fictional social media activities, such as sending WhatsApp messages (writing a script!). But a portrait can also be offered simply as text with a picture.

A classic feature draws a bow from the detailed individual case to the fundamental, "timeless": the typical form for background information that is of interest beyond the current event. The word feature originally means typical, characteristic facial or character trait. Online it often appears as a **web documentary** (formerly also: net dossier).

Virtual reality in journalism offers experiences of great immersiveness. Since the cameras are located right in the middle of the action, they transport the viewer into the middle of war zones, natural catastrophes or elaborately staged historical events, especially in reportage. Manuela Feyder and Linda Rath-Wiggins mention as fields of application for VR in journalism:

- Places to which people have no access,
- Events in the past or the future,
- Topics where a change of perspective takes place,
- Events in which people experience something that they normally do not experience themselves,
- Topics where the understanding of the story is significantly deepened when the user experiences it himself,
- Topics in which the experience is in the foreground and it is important to move at least the head to the right and left, up and down, back and front, nodding, rolling and yawing and to change position ("6-Degrees of Freedom").

For the conception of a VR contribution, they recommend a three-dimensional model in order to get a clear picture of camera positions and the audience's possibilities for action. They recommend in the handbook "VR Journalism" as planning factors for VR storytelling:

- Presence – putting yourself in the user's shoes as a visitor to the story,
- Freedom of action – consider and accept the range of options that the user can choose to experience the story,

- Spheres – the story in spheres, worlds, three-dimensional thinking as a sphere,
- Plan PoI reference points, so-called "Points of Interest",
- Perception – attracting the attention of the user,
- Assumptions – from the PoI to the next sphere and the user's behaviour and plan them,
- Relationship – the user establishes a connection to the content of the story,
- Identity – who is the user in the story? What position does he or she take? What should he identify himself with?
- Emotion – which energy reaches the user? How do the actors in the story deal with the camera? How does this affect the user? How does this feeling influence the user?
- A short video is available at http://www.gelbe-reihe.de/vr-journalismus/online-plus/, examples of VR journalism are the web documentary on Cologne Cathedral at *WDR* (https://dom360.wdr.de) or the *Süddeutsche Zeitung (South German Newspaper)* (https://gfx.sueddeutsche.de/pages/vr/).

Newsgames combine journalistic information ("news") with computer games ("games"). Cornelia Wolf and Alexander Godulla define them by the actors and the content: "Newsgames are published by media organisations and/or editorial offices working in journalism and are made available to a potentially broad public online or mobile for the reception. They make use of classic elements of game design (game rules, game mechanics, game building blocks) to process information about current or past events of social relevance. You can combine this in the game or the context of the game with Internet specifics (selectivity, multimedia, interactivity, linking). The person playing the game actively experiences processes, (background) reasons and perspectives by making selective decisions within the game." (http://journalistikon.de/newsgames).

"Prism" is a famous example of a newsgame (http://prism.thegoodevil.com) As a gamer you "help" an NSA agent to scan as many private photos as possible. You learn a lot about the US secret service and its surveillance program Prism. Since the game production requires teams of several people and longer development work, it is not easily possible to offer up to date games. These are long-term projects. Examples for newsgames can be found here: http://gamethenews.net/index.php/more-games/.

The web dossier also combines various forms of information across the media. It can consist of a report, chronicle, interview, picture gallery, original sound, short film, AR application, game and link collection. Ideally, it is based on comprehensive background research, and the user is provided with basic information about the context. Longer multimedia forms (audio, video) are also possible here.:

The right-wing extremist Oktoberfest attack of 1980, the terrorist act with the most victims in German history, is the subject of a web dossier on Bayerischer Rundfunk. At its heart is the film "Der blinde Fleck" ("The Blind Spot") based on the research of journalist Ulrich Chaussy. But the web dossier is also exciting in itself and invites you to browse through it (http://story.br.de/oktoberfest-attentat).

The entry page of the network dossier is the starting point for exploring the individual contributions. It is also the central point to which you return before you go on to explore further. Therefore, the start page of the dossier must be accessible from each individual document. Place a link to the main page on each of these pages. This is ideal if users have got lost in your system. Such a link also proves useful if surfers via search engines land somewhere deep in your site structure and want to get an overview of the entire offer first. How to design such a comprehensive online offer was described in the chapter "Hypertext".

Checklist: Inform online

This applies to all informative forms of presentation:

- The core statement in the teaser!
- Give an overview of the individual components on the homepage!
- First things first!
- Pay attention to the journalistic Ws!
- Use audio and video where text and photos are not enough!
- Background, history, charts on different pages!
- Unadulterated reproduction of facts!
- Do on-site research, not just online research!
- Do not express your own opinion!

5.4   Analyze: Commentary, Criticism, Gloss, Cartoon

The opinion is valuable: Not everyone has one that is worth reflecting on. Online, opinion occurs in various forms of communication: in chat, in forum discussions, and of course on the web. "What do you think about the so-called homosexual marriage?" asked the editors of *http://www.sueddeutsche.de* in their discussion forum. The users represent all opinions, from

> The law on registered partnership for homosexual couples is a big step towards the recognition of a minority that has suffered persecution, oppression and ridicule in the past.

as far as

> I think that gay marriage is a bunch of bullshit. And even dangerous. Marriage should
> be reserved for heterosexual couples.

Users love opinion forums. They want to vent their anger about this or that, tell the world what they think about all sorts of things and read other people's comments on their own statements. – More about this online-typical form can be found in the chapter "The participatory forms". The individual text contribution in the forum, however, falls under "opinion-oriented forms of presentation".

The introductory contribution to this discussion, written by the online editor of the discussion forum, is not itself a commentary but provides information about the disputed facts. It ends with a question:

> In the future, gay and lesbian couples will be able to live together in a legally binding
> partnership – in a kind of small marriage. For the CDU/CSU, the corresponding life
> partnership law is too similar to the legal regulations on marriage – the Gay and
> Lesbian Association, on the other hand, demands complete equality with heterosexual
> couples – including the possibility of adopting a child as a gay or lesbian couple.
> What do you think about so-called homosexual marriage?

Beyond **the simple expression of opinion** ('I find that …'), there are contributions to the discussion that address the arguments of the other side. The popular *quota* in discussion forums supports this form of debate:

> Why don't you want to recognize the way of life (gay and lesbian marriages)?
>   First of all, marriage is not a way of life. It is a legal institution. Therefore, it is not
> a question of whether or not to recognize a form of life. A lifelong monogamous
> partnership can also be legally recognised under the title of another legal form.

Journalistically structured comments are more than just the expression of opinion. They express their opinion in an orderly manner and also address counter-arguments. Above all, they analyse the situation and explain connections.

> In late autumn, it's time for self-congratulation: the cable cars and ski resorts always
> let us know what they have invested over the summer for us, the skiers and winter
> holidaymakers (…)

This is how Hans Gasser begins his commentary on winter tourism in Tyrol. From the beginning it is clear that this is about classification, about opinion – the term "self-congratulation" leaves no doubt about that. After a justification with arguments from the opposite side, the author refute these, however: neither did the skiers want this, nor does the tourism industry find enough skilled workers for the strenuous and badly paid seasonal work in the hotel and catering industry. In addition, those seeking recreation would also move away from pure skiing areas to innovative concepts. The commentary ends with a bitterly angry conclusion:

> Instead, it seems easier for many tourism actors to cover the melting glaciers with new slopes and lifts and continue as before. The main thing is that the next 20, 25 years will still pay off. After us the deluge! (Süddeutsche Zeitung, http://www.sueddeutsche.de/reise/tourismus-winter-pitztal-oetztal-skifahren-1.4688614,   accessed December 27, 2019)

This opinion can be disputed excellently – and that is exactly what makes for a good commentary. It provides arguments and challenges the user to comment. There is a lot of work behind it. Commentators have to be well versed to be able to argue competently.

Walther von La Roche distinguishes three types of comments:

1. the argumentation commentary. Example Winter Tourism
2. the straight-line commentary. Examples: the user contributions to homosexual marriage
3. the one-sided, two-sided commentary.

When commenting on a development whose outcome is uncertain, the third possibility is the one-sided, two-sided commentary. In an article for *Welt online* on how the media deal with computer games, the commentator cannot quite bring himself to find the video games indexed by the Federal Review Board for Media Harmful to Young Persons well. He does, however, point out that video games are finally recognised as a new medium and that the minor changes that now have to be made to the games for the German market are insignificant for the course of the game. His conclusion:

> As long as no one has a clever idea about this imbalance, we will remain witnesses of a strange and unique theatre in the cultural business: The players are a gigantic user and customer group, no medium has such a large audience and no one has such a striking, new influence on the other cultural sectors. At the same time, the players feel misunderstood, excluded and labelled as stupid boys – a majority as a fringe group, which now even gives vent to its anger through an association. Those who are right are not prejudiced. But that the situation is silly is unpleasantly noticeable. (http://www.welt.de/die-welt/kultur/article5421209/Videospiele-indiziert.html,   accessed December 27, 2019)

Other possible uses for the classic one-sided commentary are the upcoming elections next weekend ("the voter will decide"), the online petition that is still running, etc.

The opinion must be clearly visible. Too soft, unassailable positions do not encourage discussion. A trick: If you want to get out of the affair, get representatives of the different factions to make such comments and let them – with name and photo – represent pro and contra. Make clear length specifications so that the commentators get to the point.

Audiovisual commentaries are usually spoken by the author himself. They can be offered as audio or video. Numerous commentary formats have been created via the YouTube platform, which are also changing classic journalism online. A famous example was the YouTuber Rezo in 2019 with his contribution to the "destruction of the CDU" (https://www.youtube.com/watch?v=4Y1lZQsyuSQ).

You can write comments on any topic that is worth reporting. They are neither limited to political topics nor to necessarily take a position for one of the parties in dispute. Good commentators in particular use fact-based argumentation to find out where both parties might be mistaken and highlight aspects that have been neglected up to now.

Editorial, the topic of the day: Each department can have its own "editorial", that is, the commentary of the day: local, business, sport and others. They all comment on an important current topic, which is presented simultaneously in the news or report in a separate document. The main political commentary is called Leitartikel, analogous to the daily newspaper. It makes sense to have the topic discussed in a user forum afterwards.

The animated cartoon comments satirically on current events or general human affairs. In the simplest case, the joke lies in the fact that in a sequence of images not all of the images are shown at first so that the user is led to the moment when the punch line becomes visible. Another variant are comics controlled by the passage of time, they are shown one after the other like a slideshow and are sometimes even conceived as an infinite loop.

But the classic graphic novel can also be found online. The shortest form of annotating images is an animated GIF.

If a thing is judged and presented at the same time, one speaks of *criticism.* Reviews have a direct utility value for the user: Should I buy the book? Should I watch the film? Is the concert worth it? Should I go to this restaurant on the weekend or rather to another restaurant for dinner?

Criticism means: to describe and judge from knowledge. It contains

1. the description of content as in the case of the informative forms of presentation (report, reportage) and
2. the evaluation of content and its processing – according to the rules of the commenting forms of presentation.
3. often the service aspect is added: Is it worthwhile for the users to buy the book or CD, to attend the concert or performance?

In the construction of critique, it is by no means necessary to separate the informing and commenting parts of critique.

Criticism can be found on practically every topic. The form of book criticism or *review* is widespread. But also the big weekend contribution about the football match, the contribution about the pop concert, the theatre premiere, the excursion restaurant, even the travel report or the test report about a technical device are reviews.:

A football review. With the following teaser Focus went online:

Dortmund like in a frenzy
Borussiaaaaaaaa… 66000 fans in Dortmund's Westfalenstadion enthusiastically celebrated their stars at the Goal Festival over Wolfsburg. The team's balance after three match days: Three victories, eight goals, no conceded goal – 1st place in the league! Who else wants to stop this team? The coach warned against euphoria. …
more

In the teaser, there is hardly any evaluation – apart from the exclamation mark and the rhetorical question, which signalize: the author is not far from cheering. The mixture of information and opinion runs through the whole article. This is how the text begins:

Borussiaaaaaaaa… 66000 fans in Dortmund's Westfalenstadion enthusiastically celebrated their stars at the Goal Festival over Wolfsburg. However, coach Matthias Sammer was not able to get much out of the exuberant euphoria on the ranks of the Westfalenstadion: "After three games, the DFB does not award any titles. If we let up now for even a second, we will all experience our blue wonder," warned the BVB coach emphatically.

Opinion? No, up to this point, we're simply expressing the *coach*'s opinion. But now the evaluation of the game by the online journalist starts:

Even the impressive start with three Bundesliga victories without conceding a goal and the seemingly effortless dominance of his team in previous matches did not lure the ex-professional out of the reserve.

While the course of the game is reported, it is also commented on (reproduction of the text from 2001 slightly shortened):

Although the guest proved to be an uncomfortable opponent until the 25th minute, he lost control as the game progressed. At the latest after the 1-0 win by Amoroso, who scored his fourth goal of the season after Rosicky's spectacular pass, the tactical concept of the North Germans was no longer valid.

   Wolfgang Wolf's team even had good chances through Ponte (25th), Kühbauer (37th) and Karhan (45th), but they all missed them.

The entire description of the course of the game is aimed at the final assessment:

Both teams did not necessarily present themselves in top form, the draw was just.

Further links will bring the football fans to the right place:

Results – Goals, Goals, Goals
Table – Rostock in the cellar
Bavaria against Bavaria – A photo novel
All games – Detailed reports

A lively introduction to the article as a slide is particularly recommended in the case of reviews. Also a statement, a summarizing statement is suitable as a teaser, for the headline as well as for the lead. The statement picks out an interesting, important aspect and thus makes you curious about the detailed analysis in the following review.

   Criticism does not only mean to judge positively or negatively but above all to *establish references*. In doing so, the critic gives the user practical help in making a decision: should I buy the book, go to the film? Is the announced event suitable for children?

   Because it is particularly common online, the book review is described in more detail below.

   Book criticism is not synonymous with praise or criticism. It is much more difficult to write a precise, concise appraisal of a work that highlights strengths and does not conceal weaknesses. To do this, you have to understand something about literature, the author and the subject. If this is not the case, you have to make yourself familiar with it – not guess.

   Having read the book should be a matter of course. At the same time, note down keywords and quotations with page numbers that may be interesting for the critic, such as puns, metaphors, but also the names of the main characters, the place of the event, the period of the plot, historical references, ambiguities, even obvious mistakes.

Getting information about the author is also not difficult (blurb, publisher information, other reviews). What has he already written? What topics has his previous work covered? What literary forms has he used? How can the new work be classified here? Is the theme typical for the author, for the genre?

Getting information on the subject means a little research (search engine, special database, encyclopaedia, secondary literature). Even when writing a novel on a historical topic such as the Thirty Years' War, the reviewer should know the historical events, the historical processes. In comparison with the book, it is possible to work out where the author shortens the story to create suspense, moves the plot to a place other than the historical one, changes the characters... The same applies to a review of a textbook: not only the validity of what is presented must be examined, but also whether there is anything new, interesting or worth knowing.

Checklist for criticism in cultural journalism
A book, film, theatre or concert review should include

* a short presentation of the bid (persons, action, allusions and quotations)
* Information on the author and, if applicable, actors
* a description of the presentation
* a personal evaluation of the reviewer.

Glossary: A topic is turned and playfully turned from all sides, both linguistically and in terms of content. Because it is usually short and trenchant, the gloss is ideal for the web – provided you know a good gloss writer or are one yourself.

Two basic ideas are the minimum for a good glossary: one *linguistic* and one *substantive*. Find out what the author's basic ideas were with the following example on the subject of "bugs" (errors in computer programs):

The bugs are dying out
The bugs are dying out. And it's our fault. Can we in our conscience reconcile cruelly hunting digital creatures? WIN animal rights activist Martin Goldman demands: "Let the bugs live".

Jan from my men's group is sensitive, relativizes every second sentence with "a bit" and brakes for animals, too. The other day in the group lesson he said: "Animal love is somehow tremendously important". He's right, isn't he?

Stop: Before you nod now, think carefully about what you are raising and lowering your head for. Isn't a bug a living, sentient being? And haven't bugs been hunted, chased, killed since the first moth in the transistors burned up in agony?

The bugs are bad in our society. Thousands of beta testers throw themselves into organized hunts. Bugs are pushed further and further back into inaccessible bionics. Not even microprocessors can shelter the cute creatures. Chip manufacturers brutally etch them out of the circuits.

We have to change our thinking and finally realize Bugs are useful. They create jobs in support departments and programming rooms. They generate revenue for software companies. And let's not forget the emotional component: Bugs are responsible for a lot of the idiosyncrasies of programs Who hasn't developed loving workarounds just to not scare off their little friend? (…) Especially for the next generation, the bug must be preserved in its natural environment. Remember: We only borrowed the bugs from our children.

Protect the bugs. Install at least two Office packages on your computer – whether from Microsoft, Lotus, Corel or Star Division. Install updates only if they contain more new bugs than they remove. If you program yourself, do not test your software. Create valuable biotopes for the little friends who have been with us so faithfully since the beginning of the information age. Jan, the bugs, the men's group and I would be insanely happy.

Mastery of the linguistic peculiarities that one wants to ironically impale is a prerequisite for a glossary like this one, in which the author makes fun of the jargon of a particular scene.

In this case, the author shows that he has the animal rights rhetoric down pat, and contrasts it with the technical language of a computer magazine. So much for the basic linguistic idea – the content is based on the legend that the first computer errors were caused by moths (American: *bugs*) that invaded mainframe computers. The word "bug" has long since become a metaphor, and the author plays with it. The interlocking of beginning and end (Jan and the men's group) does the rest to round off the gloss.

Other forms of presentation that express opinions are even less defined in terms of form and structure.

Column: Regular employees, sometimes also the editor-in-chief, can have their fixed "column" (column) at regular intervals. It can be reproduced as text or even spoken by itself. Depending on temperament, the column takes up a current grievance, a discussion topic or simply something particularly silly and comments or glosses over the topic – predominantly in an entertaining way. Columns are usually offered online as a blog.

Essay: To treat a topic linguistically and in terms of content as witty as it is exhaustive, to take a stand on the great questions of the time – who wouldn't want that? The reality is different: "If you have failed something completely, call it an essay" (Kurt Tucholsky). Good essays are in short supply, and what is usually taken for it is a "dialectical reflection essay" or "discussion". The essay is the link between journalistic and literary forms. Besides mastery of the subject and language, it requires a clear statement from the author.

The online implementation of the essay poses challenges that are difficult to overcome. The main problem is the length. Spreading a well-constructed essay over several pages inhibits the flow of reading, and the overall concept is difficult to recognize. One solution would be to make the essay as a whole available for download as a PDF file, another would be to integrate it into a web dossier.

Checklist: Opinion-forming forms of the presentation online
That goes for all of them:

- Already in the teaser opinion can be seen
- Sum up the opinion
- Making your own evaluation criteria transparent
- Hold the line and prepare the punch line
- Links to background information, discussion forum, chat.

5.5   Provide Service, Write Conversion-Oriented: FAQ, Chatbot, Newsletter

Not only an opinion, but concrete advice and practical life assistance expect users on topics such as: What to do at the weekend? How do I insure myself properly? How do I make my career? Do I live healthily? How do I find the right partner? The answers are provided by *counselor journalism*. Because the benefit, the service *for the user* is in the foreground, we speak of *service texts*.

The benefit for the user lies, for example, in the answer to the question: Which refrigerator should I buy? Should I buy a book or CD, go to the event or concert, or not? Should I buy or sell the Telekom shares? What do I have to pay attention to when buying a computer? The range of service texts extends to the online course 'How to lay your garden pond properly an'.

Interaction and communication can play out their strengths here. While the readers of a magazine who have completed a questionnaire for the self-test 'Am I a good lover?', have to use a calculator to get the result, they receive the evaluation online. Anyone taking part in an electronic survey can see seconds later whether they are in the mainstream or have a marginal opinion. And on some sites, you can even initiate an online demo yourself in front of the portal of the chemical company or the political party.

The test report consists of a comparison of several products from the same division. It provides the user with comparison criteria, but also contains concrete decision-making aids. A comparison test of the organizer teast Focus online on the Digitales so homepage:

5 truths to help you extend the life of your phone battery
Smartphones are becoming increasingly powerful. In the long run, this puts a particular strain on the batteries and can have a negative effect on battery performance. Therefore, users should be particularly careful with the mobile phone battery so that the battery does not wear out unnecessarily early.

The whole topic is arranged on one long page but leads via hyperlinks to a lot of background information. (http://www.focus.de/digital/handy/tipps-fuer-langlebige-akkus-5-wahrheiten-ueber-handyakkus-schnellladen-ist-nicht-schaedlich-hitze-schon_id_11489371.html, accessed 27 December 2019).

Structure text, use enumerations. Compact pages with a visual structure are arranged for the user. Example: Under the heading 'No turning back. What tenants should watch out for' gives focus on-line compactly the most important tips for tenants and such, who want to become it:

Tenants are not bound by contract clauses that violate the law. Nevertheless, there are numerous conditions which – once signed – are irreversible. The potential new tenant should pay attention to this before placing his three crosses under a contract:
Rented rooms: Are all rooms listed, including cellar, storage, garage? If not, they are not part of the rental contract and could be used by the landlord for other things.
Contracting party: Are all residents listed in the contract? This is especially important for unmarried couples and shared flats.
Rent amount: As a rule, the net cold rent is shown here. Then, however, the additional costs appear elsewhere. Attention, if future rent increases are already stated here, as in the case of graduated or index-linked rental agreements.
Deposit: Maximum three months rent cold. Higher amounts are not allowed!

Questions and answers is a user-oriented method of dealing with the most frequently requested topics systematically and clearly. The method was developed under the name *Frequently Asked Questions (FAQ)* in discussion forums (newsgroups). The magazine *test* shows how to do this on its page on the recall action in the exhaust emissions scandal involving Opel and the VW Group (https://www.test.de/Abgasskandal-4918330-0/, accessed 28 December 2019): A special is intended to relieve the consultants at the consumer advice centres and provide the most important tips and information online. Under the heading 'FAQ exhaust gas scandal: Answers to your Fragen' the questions are listed first. Some examples:

Who is affected by the exhaust gas scandal?
What about other manufacturers?
What happens to scandal cars?
What is politics doing in the emissions scandal?
How do I find out which emission class my car has?

> The car manufacturers offer "environmental bonuses" if you return your old diesel. Is it worth it? (…)

As there are quite a lot of questions, the editors have divided them into blocks such as Retrofitting – Manipulated wagons – Customer rights etc. The eye can see them better.

Each question leads to an anchor in the following continuous text, example:

> How do I find out which emission class my car has?
> The pollutant class, for example 'Euro 4', shall be indicated on the registration certificate (box 14).

Directly addressing the user is another way to get rid of advice and tips. 'How to save inheritance tax', Focus online teases out a whole collection of tips on wills and inheritance. Each editorial office has internal guidelines on how to address the user personally. Some bypass them and save themselves in constructions such as 'If you want to save taxes, you should …' Others consciously use the style of the advisor: 'Pay attention when buying …, Never conclude contracts without comparing prices …'

Bots, mostly chatbots, are used **in journalism** as well as in other customer services. The bot is given a *persona*, an identity that is as close as possible to the target group. The texts are short and easy to understand. Markus Kaiser, the author of "Journalistische Praxis: Chatbots", advises to provide several response options when writing the dialogue trees and to avoid "dead ends".

> Give the bot an identity, a so-called *persona* – a name, a face, a biography.

A bot is therefore an interface that sends answers to requests. Therefore it is also called a conversational interface. Software developers program bots using a bot framework.

The bot consists of the underlying logic (an if-then system) as well as a bot connector, which is connected to any channel via an API (interface) without setting up the corresponding programming language for the respective channel.

For the bot to react correctly and continue learning, it must be trained. *Human Teaching* and *Machine Learning* are suitable for this.

With the increasing use of speech recognition software and voice dialogues, voice chat offers are gaining in importance.

With questionnaires that are immediately evaluated online, personal contact is usually unavoidable. The following example calculates the exceptional charges that can be claimed for tax purposes. It comes again from Focus online:

Total amount of your annual income:
(Please enter without dot and space)
They are
( ) single
( ) married
and have children
Calculate

Clear prompts for input are necessary. A question like 'Do you rarely smoke or häufig' with

( ) yes
( ) no

does not exactly show precision.

The direct approach is also **gender-appropriate**. It does not interrupt the flow of reading and thus represents an elegant alternative to the usual solutions with "gender star", the underscore "gender gap" or the slash solution used in this book, combined with gender-neutral formulations ("in the online editorial office …").

You have to find out for yourself **which questions move your audience.** Numerous calls are answered by the questionnaire of "Dr. Longlife", a self-test of your own living habits, which is offered on http://www.sueddeutsche.de. The headline reads: 'Calculate how old you will become!' If users answer questions like these, they will finally receive the evaluation, measured against the average life expectancy of the population:

Do you exercise regularly?

( ) yes
( ) no

   Are you unemployed?

( ) yes
( ) no

Surveys are another interactive way to offer your users action offers including exclusive information. The highlight lies in the evaluation that each user receives as soon as they have sent their answers to the server. This is how the Süddeutsche online asks:

Should conscription be abolished?

( ) yes
( ) no

The surprising result: 73% of the respondents voted "yes" and 26% "no" in August 2001. A total of 962 votes were cast by the time we tested the survey.

E-learning requires those who design such self-learning courses not only to master the subject matter but also to prepare it didactically. This goes beyond journalistic forms of presentation. The author must decide which methods and which media use (text, audio, video, forum, chat?) are best suited to convey the material.

Knowledge is **conveyed online in** various ways. While some students choose the time and place of learning themselves, others log on to the computer several times a week for a set time. Lessons are taught via hypertext, but also in the classic classroom conversation: via chat, audio, video. The lecturers explain the material using presentation slides. Success is in any case dependent on the self-discipline of the users.

E-learning offers usually consist **of prepared information in hypermedia,** diagrams, audio and video sequences, reference works (e.g. encyclopaedia of technical terms in this book and online), bibliographic information and self-learning elements up to quizzes and games. Mountains of text provided in PDF format, filmed, recorded lectures or classroom events have nothing to do with e-learning except as a supplement. Special importance is attached to exercises specially prepared for the screen.

Depending on the topic, there are various ways of **checking whether a user has achieved the learning goal**: Standardized knowledge can be conveniently queried online, similar to self-tests. More complex knowledge and skills cannot be learned and practiced by multiple choice but must be processed and controlled with the help of participative forms.

Frequent communication contacts deepen the relationship between the users and increase the learning effect. In this way, learning groups can communicate their results to each other and provide feedback. Questions arising during the solution can be discussed in regularly held *chats*, see the chapter "The participative forms".

For more complex topics, only classical supervision and individual coaching by the lecturers can help. The combination of presence learning and e-learning is called *blended learning*.

Intensive attendance phases at the beginning and end of the project increase the success rate of e-learning offerings. Pure distance learning offers often have an extremely high dropout rate. Because e-learning is usually designed for longer periods of time, it requires a clear structure and a chronologically logical structure.

Electronic newsletters end up in the user's e-mail inbox via e-mail distribution lists. A discussion among the users is not intended. However, feedback on each issue of the newsletter should be provided for – most simply by means of a newsletter header or footer in which the most important data (imprint, author, contact address) are integrated.

Newsletter as a marketing instrument: Because newsletters are a classic broadcasting medium similar to a subscribed newspaper or magazine, they are well suited to draw users' attention to the news in their own online magazine. Newspapers such as "Süddeutsche" or "Zeit" send out newsletters on request at regular intervals, which draw attention to the top topics of the printed edition. Radio and television stations offer similar services.

Whether your newsletter is distributed for a fee or free of charge, whether it contains advertising or not, you can decide based on the market situation and your information and marketing goals.

Technically, the information is sent by e-mail to a distribution station, which then forwards it to all users entered in the distribution list.

In the simplest case, you can also use your own in-house mail program as a distribution station: Almost all of them offer a "list" or "distribution list" function. Disadvantage: You have to maintain this distribution list manually, automatic entry and removal are not possible for the users. This effort can only be made with very small user numbers. Numerous providers provide professional newsletter solutions.

Autonomy for the user means for newsletters as well as for mailing lists: Only users who are really interested in your newsletter receive it; the others can *unsubscribe* themselves from the mailing list with a simple command. It is recommended that you also allow an open subscription to the newsletter (*subscribe*) via your website.

If the user can choose between two versions of the newsletter, one with pure text and one with a visual presentation (HTML or more), you offer even more autonomy. The trend is towards newsletters with an attractive layout and hypertext and multimedia elements.

Hypertext per newsletter: The special charm of a newsletter lies in setting links, also to cross-media offers. Even in pure text newsletters, they can be clicked on. HTML newsletters, on the other hand, open up all the possibilities that a good start page for an online magazine offers.

How you decide, whether for the multi-page newsletter with page-internal anchors or for a newsletter with teasers that lead to your web pages immediately when clicked (see the chapter "Hypertext"), is a question of strategy. In the first case, you help the user to save transmission costs. In the second case, you increase the number of hits on your website. Advertising success can be achieved with both forms of advertising: with high subscriber numbers on the one hand, with many *page impressions* or *visits on the* other.

Structure, content, style. The first screen of the newsletter also provides an overview of the entire content, preferably with meaningful headline teasers. From the print sector, the newsletter is known as a concise, compact information carrier of a few pages, often containing advice or service elements. A business newsletter, for example, provides information on economic topics such as the development of share prices or tips on how to increase sales. Online, on the other hand, some newsletters are especially appreciated for their biting short comments or glosses.

All online forms of the newsletter have one thing in common: sooner or later, external links lead to the online offer of the newsletter sender. Therefore, the basics of hypertext writing, as taught in the hypertext chapter, are directly transferable to the newsletter.

Organization and archiving. The newsletter is ideal for publishing teasers and texts one more time. From the news that appears on your online offer, you can take over a selection in the daily or weekly newsletter. Part of this editorial work can be easily automated. That is why you should think about the use of a suitable *editorial system* that takes websites, newsletters and archiving into account as early as the conception of a newsletter.

In this way, you can build up a news archive including additional documents parallel to the dispatch of the current newsletter. Depending on your strategy, you can open your newsletter archive online only for a small circle (subscribers) or for all users.

What was said **for the teasers** in the chapter "Hypertext" is also true here: The newsletter entries should (1) summarize and inform, (2) ask questions and (3) arouse curiosity and announce.

Newsletter texts are usually **conversion-oriented**: either they lead to a website – or they encourage the purchase of a product or service. This is where the border to advertising language begins. Since conversion-oriented writing is also playing an increasingly important role in online editorial marketing, here are a few brief tips.

Conversion means: "to turn a prospective buyer into a buyer". The conversion rate is calculated from the ratio of purchases per visitor. The absolute value can sometimes be more meaningful than the ratio alone. Conversion tracking measures the effectiveness with which the target group is persuaded to carry out the desired action.

The classic: AIDA.
The classic AIDA formula from marketing helps with conversion:

- Attention: attract attention
- Interest: grab at the interests
- Desire: "want to have"
- Action: → click

Once **again, the target group analysis helps** to address the target group in the right way. Who is the site aimed at? The language level is derived from this, including whether the users are addressed by their first name or by their first name. **Why continue reading?** Use the teaser to highlight the value of use, as the City of Munich does here with tips on saving heating costs in its information portal for citizens (Fig. 5.4).
Conversion-oriented writing

Die ultimativen Heiz- und Warmwassertipps

Everyone wants to pay less for heating. But which tips can save you the most money? And what's the easiest way to avoid CO2 emissions with smart heating? The Bauzentrum München reveals which savings tricks really help you.

Tip #1
Use electronic thermostats
How does it sound? When you get up in the morning, your

Tip #2
Reduce room temperature
Whether the living room is 20 degrees or 21 degrees Celsius.

Fig. 5.4 Saving heating costs

This applies to all service texts:

- write in the language of the target group
- Do not presuppose technical terms, but explain them; offer a glossary
- address the users directly
- emphasize the value of utility
- actively formulate, it is not recommended, but the consumer advice centre advises
- call upon sb. to act
- Use interactive (questionnaires) and communication (send us an e-mail! Ask our expert in the chat …)

Further Reading

1. Christoph Fasel: Textsorten. Cologne: Herbert von Halem 2013
2. Gabriele Hooffacker, Klaus Meier: La Roche's Introduction to Practical Journalism (Journalistische Praxis), Wiesbaden: Springer VS, current edition
3. Axel Buchholz, Katja Schupp (eds.), Television Journalism (Journalistische Praxis), Wiesbaden: Springer VS, current edition
4. Andreas Butz, Heinrich Hußmann, Rainer Malaka: Medieninformatik. Munich: Pearson Studium 2009
5. Walther von La Roche, Axel Buchholz (eds.), Radio Journalism (Journalistische Praxis), Wiesbaden: Springer, current edition, selected articles: http://www.radio-journalismus.de
6. Gunther Rothfuss et al.: Content Management mit XML. Berlin: Springer (current edition)
7. Björn Staschen: Mobile Journalism (Journalistische Praxis), Wiesbaden: Springer VS 2017
8. Anja M. Hoppe, Glossenschreiben. A handbook for journalists. Opladen: Westdeutscher Verlag 2000
9. Werner Nowag/Edmund Schalkowski, Kommentar und Glosse. Cologne: Herbert von Halem 1998
10. Gunter Reus, Department: Feuilleton: Cultural Journalism for Mass Media (2nd, revised edition, UVK, Konstanz 1999)
11. Barbara Brandstetter: Verbraucherjournalismus. Cologne: Herbert von Halem 2014
12. Markus Kaiser et al.: Journalistic Practice: Chatbots. Wiesbaden: Springer VS 2019
13. Markus Kaiser (ed.): Special Interest: Ressortjournalismus – Konzepte, Ausbildung, Praxis. Wiesbaden: Springer VS 2012

Further Links

14. Selfhtml e. V., http://www.selfhtml.org (retrieved 27 December 2019)
15. https://www.gelbe-reihe.de

Further Literature (Selection)

16. Axel Buchholz, Katja Schupp (eds.), Television Journalism (Journalistische Praxis), Wiesbaden: Springer VS, current edition
17. Manuela Feyder, Linda Rath-Wiggins: VR Journalism (Journalistische Praxis), Wiesbaden: Springer VS 2018
18. Walther von La Roche, Axel Buchholz (eds.), Radio Journalism (Journalistische Praxis), Wiesbaden: Springer, current edition, selected articles: http://www.radio-journalismus.de
19. Mario Müller-Dofel: Conducting Interviews (Journalistische Praxis), Wiesbaden: Springer VS, current edition

Participatory Forms and Formats

6

Abstract

Users can basically do two things online: first, they can retrieve predefined information, i.e. interact with a server (see the previous chapter), and second, they can interact with other users and the online editorial team. The forms that focus on communication with other users are what I call the *participatory forms*. In earlier editions of the textbook, they were called "communicative forms" to distinguish them from purely broadcast-oriented journalistic forms of presentation.

6.1   Online: Participation and Collaboration

In online journalism, the audience, as shown in the first chapter, leaves the passive role of the "lean back" to an active role, it switches between the communicator and the recipient role. Digital journalism offers numerous possibilities to let the audience participate in journalistic products, up to the independent creation and production of contributions.

Communication scientist Wiebke Loosen explores such new possibilities of inclusion of journalism and audience.[1] "The future of professional journalism could lie in the intelligent inclusion of the audience," Christoph Neuberger, a pioneer of digital communication, wrote back in 2012.[2] At HTWK Leipzig (Leipzig University

---

[1] Wiebke Loosen: Audience participation in journalism. In K. Meier, & C. Neuberger, *Journalism research* (2 eds., pp. 287–318). Baden-Baden: Nomos 2016.

[2] Christoph Neuberger: Citizen Journalism as a Solution? Empirical Results on the Journalistic Performance of Lay Communication. In O. Jarren, M. Künzler, & M. Puppis, *Media*

© Springer Fachmedien Wiesbaden GmbH, part of Springer Nature 2022   123
G. Hooffacker, *Online journalism*,
https://doi.org/10.1007/978-3-658-35731-3_6

of Applied Sciences), we are experimenting with participatory formats, for example in local TV journalism.[3]

Is there any interest at all in participation **on the part of the audience**? Who is eligible for it? What types of participation are conceivable? The change in technical production conditions makes all kinds of gradations of participation possible, from giving ideas for research to regular "broadcasting" of videos.

So-called "citizen journalism" occupies an intermediate stage in this process. Born in the 1970s out of dissatisfaction with the mass media, it initially led to the founding of so-called alternative media. It came into focus again with the protest movements of the 2010s from the right.

Since then, actors in online and social media editorial offices have been striving to explain the journalistic approach and methodology to their audience on the one hand, and to involve them in the production of journalistic contributions on the other. Instead of the term "citizen journalism", I prefer the English term "citizen journalists", which focuses on participation in media and society.

Five layers of participatory involvement
can be distinguished.

Layer 1: Crowdsourcing for topic identification and research
The online editorial team asks citizens to contribute to an existing topic. This content is recorded in databases and processed visually. The contribution of individuals is hardly visible here. This form is typical for *data journalism*.

Layer 2: Add-on reporting
The audience provides information and material – text, images, audio, video – on a specific topic or event. The online editorial team checks the supplied material for factual accuracy and plausibility and incorporates it into the article. Here, too, the editorial team sets the topic; the possibly lower quality of the supplied material is negligible, as it is edited.

Layer 3: Citizen journalism with editorial support
In consultation with the editorial team, the citizens choose their topic. They research and produce journalistic material. The online editorial team checks it and builds a contribution from it. This form of collaboration requires close cooperation between citizen reporters and the editorial team, such as regular participation in editorial meetings. It places higher demands on the online journalistic skills of the audience, but also on editorial support.

Layer 4: Bloghouse – space for the audience

---

change or media crisis? Implications for media structures and their study (pp. 53–76). Baden-Baden: Nomos 2012.

[3] Gabriele Hooffacker: Citizen Reporters: Between Participation and Professional Editing. Formats of citizen journalism in local television. In: Journalistik 3/2018, https://journalistik. online/en/paper-en/citizenreporting-between-participation-and-professional-journalism/, retrieved December 28, 2019.

In the form of blogs or podcasts, citizen journalists are provided with fixed spaces for publication. They fill these independently with a contribution ready for publication. So there is a lot of freedom for the design; at the same time, the demands on the citizen reporters are high. For the viewers, the blog or vlog is recognizable as a participatory format.

Layer 5: Editorially independent citizen journalism

Entire contributions on freely selectable topics that are ready for publication come from the audience. The editorial team's technology and platform can be used, and the editorial team can specify topics. The audience thus becomes the producer. For the online editors, this entails a certain risk in terms of topic selection and quality; for citizen journalists, the high degree of independence is very attractive.

Previous editorial attempts suggest as a conclusion that online editors would like to see contributions produced as promptly and professionally produced as possible, i.e. participation in the sense of layer 5 "editorially independent *citizen journalism*" identified above.

The mostly voluntarily committed from sports or local cultural associations often cannot afford this daily, professional online journalism – even if they want to. They see their possibilities more in layer 3, an "citizen journalism with editorial support". Here, they provide material; the editorial team checks and edits it and finishes the article.

On the other hand, the format of layer 4, "bloghouse – space for the audience", has turned out to be a compromise accepted by both sides. A fixed publication space is available for this. For the audience, the vlog is recognizable as a participatory format. There is a lot of freedom for design; at the same time, the demands on the citizen reporters to work independently are high.

For participatory forms and formats to succeed, there are three prerequisites that can be derived from previous experience:

1. There must be an interest among the participants from the audience to create publicity for the topic. In order to take on a journalistic task, an intrinsic motivation to contribute something to the topic is indispensable. At the same time, the editorial team has the task of ensuring a balance of interests and inclusive reporting.
2. The technical hurdle must be as low as possible in order to prevent participants from losing their desire to participate. A prolonged involvement with technical processes such as registration, activation, etc. is perceived as disruptive.
3. The control over the publication must lie with the participants. They would have to be able to decide for themselves when a content should no longer be seen, for example, if it has lost its topicality and thus its relevance is diminished.

Crowd-based data journalism is one way to implement layer 1. It is based on the so-called *Internet of Things*. Data journalism is classically understood as the visualization of structured statistical data sets that are based on a socially relevant question. Data wrapping tools are used for this purpose. How does the division of Germany still affect us decades later? In response, *Zeit online* has compiled talking, often curious graphics (http://www.zeit.de/feature/mauerfall-das-geteilte-land, retrieved December 28, 2019).

An example from local journalism: You can use citizens to do research and evaluate the whole thing digitally. The *Tagesspiegel* has equipped a hundred cyclists from different Berlin districts with digital distance meters and evaluated the result. The result: The fewest car drivers keep the minimum distance when overtaking (http://www.tagesspiegel.de/berlin/projekt-radmesser-so-gefaehrlich-werden-radfahrer-in-berlin-ueberholt/23702706.html, retrieved December 28, 2019).

Journalism of things or sensor journalism uses sensors that collect data distributed among the users. Jacob Vicari describes the *Harlem Heat Project* in his book of the same name. The sensor journalist John Keefe implemented it together with *New York Public Radio*.

The study was based on the hypothesis that poorer populations in Harlem suffer more from heat waves than wealthier ones because they cannot afford air conditioning and thermal insulation. Citizens were given homemade sensors that recorded data every 15 minutes. These then had to be transmitted by hand. Result: In many apartments, the indoor temperature index was significantly higher than in the surrounding area. Urban planning can react to this.

The spectrum of participatory formats ranges from individual communication via *direct messaging, instant messaging and social media platforms* with their multimodal possibilities to collaborative (joint) data collection and writing in *wikis* or games in virtual worlds.

In between are forms such as *blogs, podcasts, microblogging* and other services that combine the distribution of individually generated content (text, images, audio, video) with subscription, feedback (commentary) and other networking opportunities. Their precursors are mailing lists, forums or groups,

In online communities and social networks, several of these forms are usually combined into participatory formats:

- *Individual communication* via direct message and instant messaging.
- *Apps* that are filled with data by users and evaluated collectively.
- *Communities* that offer the usual *social signals* such as *like* or *share* for the media content.

- Platforms that allow, for example, closed rooms or groups for *virtual confer-ences.*
- *Cloud-based collaboration.*
- *Virtual worlds* as in multiplayer online games.

The online medium mediates this communication.

In terms of **online journalism**, these participatory forms are interesting when they are integrated into an overall media format. The *difference* between an open chat and an online journalistic chat can be compared to the difference between a conversation in a stairwell and a conversation in a talk show.

As with other media, we distinguish between *synchronous* or "live" forms and *asynchronous* or time-delayed forms. Chat belongs to the "live" forms; blogs, fo-rums, mailing lists and newsletters to the time-delayed, asynchronous forms. Within this classification, a distinction can again be made between pure broadcast forms (newsletters) and participative forms (mailing lists, forums). For this reason, you will find the topic of newsletters in the previous article "Forms of presenta-tion".

6.2   Social Media Platforms

This chapter begins with an overview of social media (also: Web 2.0) and then fol-lows the increasing complexity of participatory forms: From *e-mail* and *instant messaging* to *Skype*, from *blogs* and *forums,* the other contributions are about.

One speaks of an online community, if the participative forms together with the interactive ones, the synchronous ones with the asynchronous ones, result in a coherent overall concept for a clearly defined target group. The last article in this chapter deals with the objectives, conception, maintenance and care of such a com-munity and the management of user-generated content.

Under the catchword social media or *Web 2.0*, the participative online formats have been summarized since about 2004. The buzzword Web 2.0 was intended to describe the media-specific possibilities of online communication. In contrast to the World Wide Web, which only in retrospect was called "Web 1.0", the number-ing of versions familiar from software marketing was intended to suggest a qualita-tive leap towards "Web 2.0".

Under Web 2.0, all types of *user-generated content* (UGC) are summarized online. This includes the technologies that are necessary for collaboration on the web as well as the associated business models. There is no clear scientific defini-tion. Other related terms around Web 2.0 are "social web", "semantic web", "social networks" or "social media" (unfortunate, but very common translation of "social media") up to participative or collaborative formats online.

In terms of programming, Web 2.0 is characterized by technologies such as JavaScript, JavaServer-Pages and PHP, AJAX, RSS and XML-based web services (Behrendt p. 4 ff.). (Behrendt 2008: 4 ff.).

The fundamental change that has actually taken place in digital journalism has been illustrated by Christoph Neuberger in Fig. 6.1.

Where once only online editors decide what information was offered to the public, today the users themselves can actively and interactively participate in the exchange of information and opinions. The role of journalists as gatekeepers has

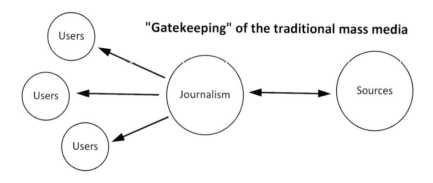

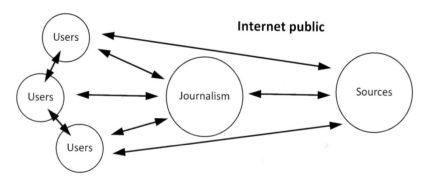

Fig. 6.1 Change in digital journalism. (After Klaus Meier: Journalistik, Konstanz: utb 2018)

changed. Previously, the traditional media were considered gatekeepers who decided what was published and what was not.

The change was first seen in the so-called blogosphere, i.e. the weblogs.
Christoph Neuberger says: "No other medium allows providers to respond so flex-
ibly to user expectations. However, users do not provide editors with ready-made
blueprints, but only suggestions that have to be interpreted and implemented professionally" (Fig. 6.2).

Characteristic of social media are combinations of participatory forms with
other applications such as geo-tagging or collaborative rating and indexing of content. Also typical is the increasing use of video elements in the context of communities such as TikTok, Snapchat and of course YouTube, where collaborative tagging and rating is characteristic, combined with further applications on the social
media platforms.

The use of social media platforms represents a return to content produced by
users, who thus become "prosumers". Long before the invention of the World Wide
Web, such content in instant messaging, chats and forums formed the first applications of the Internet. The term "Web 2.0" became known through Tim O'Reilly,
founder of the publishing house of the same name, and his article "What is Web
2.0" published at the end of September 2005. Typical Web 2.0 applications include

Interview with Stefan Aigner on the subject of blog

PRESSEFREIHEIT WELTWE

Fig. 6.2 Stefan Aigner on his journalistic blogging activities for regensburg.digital.de
(https://www.gelbe-reihe.de/online-journalismus/stefan-aigner/ or directly https://youtu.be/
xS-VHElQCXg)

blogs, wikis as well as third-party platforms such as Facebook, Twitter, Instagram or TikTok, media-specific platforms such as YouTube or Soundcloud, and platforms with specific functions such as Xing or LinkedIn. Blog technology, a simplified content management system (CMS) for chronologically sorted entries, made it easy for anyone with Internet access to publish content on the Web and network with each other without knowledge of HTML. By separating content, structure and design, the XML concept allowed subscribing to so-called news feeds (RSS or ATOM). This made regularly updated content possible as a blog or podcast in the pull rather than push principle.

The most popular Wiki CMS is that of Wikimedia, which is behind the online encyclopedia Wikipedia. It started in 2001 and is one of the top five most visited websites in the world in 2019. All contributions are created collaboratively by users with graded rights. At the same time, Wikipedia provides a prime example of the difficulties that this method of working entails: a high attrition rate of active users, so-called edit wars for the sovereignty of interpretation of certain terms, and the phenomenon of "sock puppets", accounts behind which users hide under pseudonyms who may be on the platform more than once.

Third-party platforms such as the US companies Facebook or Twitter Inc. also emerged since the mid-noughties. On or the Chinese company Bytedance (TikTok) rose to become global players.

Data protectionists criticize the business model in which users virtually pay with their data. Media companies that work with third-party platforms must take this into account.

The demand for an independent platform, managed by the users themselves, has been around for a long time. What would media formats and platforms have to do to advance a digitized, diverse society? A suggestion:

1. The participatory platforms belong to themselves, not to any corporation. They are "non-profit" and could be organised in a decentralised and cooperative way.
2. The platforms combine classic media topics and content with content and media formats created by the citizens themselves.
3. They provide access to classic media via a distribution model based on a flat rate, similar to "Netflix" for films or "Steam" for games.
4. The users set the rules for the discourse themselves. Everyone decides for themselves what they want to reveal about themselves and what not.
5. Transparent algorithms regulate data protection and data security.

The Fediverse represents an approach in this direction. It is based on open software and aims to allow its users to access all "federated" social networks without having to register themselves. It is enough to have an account with just one of them. This is implemented through shared protocols such as *OStatus* or *ActivityPub*. It remains to be seen whether the concept will catch on.

However the term Web 2.0 originated, it definitely comes from marketing. That is why it is so vague and imprecise to define: On the one hand, Web 2.0 describes *user-generated content,* the active participation of Internet users and the exchange of information between them. On the other hand, Web 2.0 stands for a combination of technical developments that became usable from 2004 onwards due to larger bandwidths: intelligent programming interfaces such as web service APIs, Ajax, subscription services with RSS, or the so-called social software such as *social bookmarking* and *folksonomies* ("folksonomy": portmanteau of "folks" and "taxonomy"), blogs, Twitter, wikis.

The term Web 2.0 has now been replaced by terms such as "social media" or "social networks". For journalism, participatory formats are becoming increasingly important online.

Community indexing (social tagging) is a form of free tagging (indexing) in which users assign keywords (tags) to content. Several *tags* together form a *tag cloud.*

The folksonomy is mainly used on websites or in the communities they offer in order to keyword and rate their content. Other users then find this weighted information by searching for a keyword. Examples: blog entries, photos or social bookmarks.

Why should online editors engage on social media platforms? As the ARD-ZDF online study shows, more than two-thirds of all German online users spend a lot of time there. The platforms offer very good opportunities for user engagement. They are crucial for the perception (attention) and reception of content. They bring further users to one's own content – also by contributing to search engine optimization. In addition, their success can be measured well in social signals (share, like, comment).

What goals do users associate with social media? Stefan Primbs distinguishes between three functions:

1. Relationship management: The intensity of relationships ranges from Facebook friending as a substitute for exchanging business cards to close exchanges within the family and circle of friends.
2. Information management: On Facebook or Twitter, I find out what is interesting for me, my friends, my colleagues. I do not have to actively search for news and current information, they reach me there through my circle of acquaintances or subscriptions.

3. Identity management: With my postings, I create a (better) image of myself, create an image for myself.

From these, rules for successful social media posts can be derived: What content do social media users want to show up with in front of their network? What content would they like to share with them? (Fig. 6.3).

Successful posts cover content that is likely to meet with approval. This includes witty, entertaining posts. On the other hand, content that users and their network will have a similar attitude towards. This can be happy, emotional content, or occasionally content that the network agrees to disagree with.

A meme is when the visual design of a post quotes and develops familiar themes or images in an appealing, witty way. For example, millions of social media users know (and love) "Grumpy Cat" or the popular proverbial cat videos.

Successful posts or memes are usually

- funny/witty
- easy to grasp intellectually
- meeting with approval in the social environment of the fans (no one shares something that their friends find repulsive)
- get to the point quickly (for videos: omit the introduction)
- "sexy", attractive
- surprisingly
- positive and highly emotional/touching/concerning (babies, animals, fates, catastrophes)
- with a good accompanying text.

Fig. 6.3 Thomas Leidel of NTV.de via social media (https://www.gelbe-reihe.de/online-journalismus/thomas-leidel/ or directly https://soundcloud.com/user-115120916/das-geheimnis-guter-arbeit-ist-die-eigene-motivation)

The story format comprises several short video clips that together tell a story. It was originally created on the Snapchat platform. In the meantime, it has evolved from an ephemeral format whose content is deleted after 24 hours to an archivable audiovisual format on numerous social media platforms, including Instagram and also Facebook. Classically, it is produced and also transmitted with the smartphone.

To make the story format work,

- Plan starting point
- Plan final point
- Engage followers
- Receive feedback
- Use reporter personality
- Stay information-oriented.

The story format lends itself to live reporting when situations change repeatedly over a period of time and different people are available as interviewees. The reporter can be in the picture in a "selfie look". However, the people and scenes that are transmitted at intervals under a fixed hashtag arouse considerably more interest. The individual clips can later be used to create classic reports.

Copywriting for social media posts? What Walther von La Roche described for radio language can be transferred well to language for AV media:

- Theme (what is known) forward, rheme (what is new) thereafter
- No subordinate clauses
- Use common words
- Repetitions are not only allowed, but facilitate understanding
- Forward verb
- Use carefully: metaphors, puns, irony (usually not understood)

Subtitles for social media videos also follow these rules. In the case of news-based video clips, they do not follow the spoken text in full, but reproduce it in abbreviated form. The core statements must be preserved. In this way, the clip is also understandable for those who are currently on the move without headphones.

So-called mashups combine such applications with additional content such as text, data, images, sounds or videos. The mashups use the open programming interfaces (APIs) provided by other web applications. Using the Google Maps API, for example, you can integrate maps and satellite photos on your own website and also add individual markers.

Dirk von Gehlen, online journalist and innovation researcher, has described the mashup as the basis of cultural networking. And Jan-Hinrik Schmidt, in his standard work "Social Media", sees the participatory and networking potential of the Internet as a reflection of networked societies: "We live in a society of networked individuality. The Internet, and social media in particular, are the perfect technologies for this form of society."

6.3   Individual Communication Online

No, this little chapter is not about how to write business emails (although that certainly would not hurt). It just wants to make you aware that online individual communication mixes with public communication. Suddenly your editorial WhatsApp messages end up in a thread on a public social media platform after all, privacy protection or not. So here are just a few quick recommendations for editorial communication.

Mailing lists serve the exchange between users with similar interests. Similar to the newsletter, the individual contributions are delivered to the user's own e-mail inbox after he or she has decided to subscribe to the mailing list. In contrast to the newsletter, feedback from the list participants is not only desired, but an essential part of this form.

Among the asynchronous forms, the direct message between online journalist and user is still of great importance. E-mails usually reach users immediately. Enabling direct e-mail contact between editor and user, however, also means making a considerable amount of time available for this purpose. This effort is rewarded with a direct "ear" to the user – the best *market research* imaginable.

In marketing, the importance of e-mail should also not be underestimated. Just as the behaviour of an employee on the phone has long been regarded as an "acoustic business card", emails to users should fit in with the overall communication concept of the site. The e-mail a user receives from an online journalist shapes his or her perception of the entire product. It is the best guarantee for a successful user-site connection.

Organizationally, it can make sense to channel the mail traffic with the user. Technically, there are many ways to do this – from a general e-mail address for letters to the editor to separate "user mail accounts" to a service center with a ticket system that handles standard inquiries. However, they cannot replace direct contact between the online editor and the user. In any case, all e-mails should be archived so that past correspondence can be referred to in case of doubt.

An email etiquette guide within the editorial team is one way of ensuring that all members of the editorial team send e-mails that meet certain formal and content-related criteria. Text modules for standard queries or documents made available via the intranet help to keep the burden on online editors to a minimum.

Subject: The "subject" or topic has a function between headline and teaser in the e-mail. A subject 'Information' is meaningless, better would be the concrete topic: 'How our chatroom works'.

The answer should be factual and formulated in a friendly style. Resist the temptation to make fun of the user's request in reply e-mails (even if it sometimes makes you itch). Whether it is clumsy wording or simply a lack of practice with the medium, help rather than mock. One disgruntled user can do a lot of damage through word of mouth.

To unfriendly direct mails, a factual answer is easy to say. As a journalist, you are on the road professionally. In a professional context, write in such a way that your text could be published at any time – even if your counterpart did not comply.

Please do not send **too large files as attachments** by e-mail, newsletter or mailing list. Not all users are as comfortably connected to the online medium as you are in your editorial department! Instead, send a download link to a platform such as WeTransfer or similar.

Not time-delayed, but live (synchronous), the following forms can be used. The following applies to all of them: they have only been triumphant since the beginning of the twenty-first century, since affordable *flat rates* have been available and since telephone charges and online access in general have become significantly cheaper. It is therefore not presumptuous to predict a great future for these forms of communication.

On the community spirit of an online magazine,
the direct connection between users and with the online editorial team is one of the most important aspects. More and more media are encouraging their employees to have direct contact with the user via e-mail, forum, instant messaging, chat or webcam. Especially from this point of view, such participative, synchronous forms find their way into this handbook.

Instant messaging (IM) via text, audio or video is comparable to e-mail because of the personal communication. Unlike e-mail, however, users can communicate *peer-to-peer* not only in pairs, but also with several others via service providers. The platform often shows who of the circle of friends is currently online. This is questionable from a data protection point of view.

The most famous became *Skype*. Many interviews are conducted via Skype. They can be digitally recorded and further processed, although the technical quality leaves something to be desired.

Data protection is not enthusiastic about the possibilities of permanent controllability – not even about the security risk that arises when a company's own firewalls are penetrated. A firewall is a technical security measure that is supposed to ward off foreign access to one's own data as well as virus attacks. Any holes in the security system are potentially dangerous.

Apart from that, mandatory attendance is annoying: Online journalists should ensure that they are not constantly reachable, but have the option of taking time out and using digital "answering machines" – most IM programs offer this option as well.

The chat today usually takes place via a web interface. The model from the early days of the *Internet*, the *Internet relay chat* (irc), still exists. Channels, similar to CB radio, ensure that the various target groups and their topics do not get in each other's way. It is also possible to open your own channel at certain times and occasions – all you have to do is give the channel a descriptive name. Platforms such as *Discord* also offer these possibilities.

In the partial anonymity of the participants, the appeal of chatting lies in the fact that people communicate directly and often unmoderated with each other. A certain adherence to the rules of the game is ensured by programs that automatically filter out certain words with the help of a stop word list *(badlist)* and editors who monitor the course of the chat from time to time.

In contrast to this is the moderated chat, which resembles a moderated news broadcast or a technical discussion: Usually an *expert* is invited, who is available in a certain period of time. A moderator collects the questions from the users, arranges and tightens them or even allows questions directly. Such expert discussions are usually recorded and are also available to the users at a later time for reading on the website. If your online offer is an extension of a parent medium, plan the chat in close cooperation with its editorial team: If there is a travel special, invite the travel law expert who was interviewed there into the chat; if a pop group is the studio guest, listeners or viewers can chat with the musicians afterwards.

Mobile live cams prove the authenticity of what is shown: Now, at this minute, the Oktoberfest is really opening in Munich; the radio presenter and her interlocutor are really sitting in the studio. Combined with the chat, journalists and users exchange pictures and videos via smartphone.

6.4   Ancestors: Blogs, Microblogging, Forums

What roles does blogging and tweeting play for online journalism? Certainly not every blogger is a journalist. But many journalists blog and tweet. On the one hand, it may bring awareness and an image boost. On the other hand, it is simply fun to try out the possibilities of the online medium without having to submit to the strict journalistic rules. Because with the forums since the 1980s, the blogs since the end of the 1990s and Twitter since 2006, fundamental forms of online communication have emerged in each case, here is an excursion to the very lively ancestors. (Blogs and forums were, by the way, already a topic in the first edition of this handbook in 2001.)

In many blogs, written by journalistic laymen – but perhaps experts in their field – facts, topics and opinions can be found that do not (yet) appear in the classic media – an exciting field of research. Blogs are located between the classical media and citizen journalism: a journalistic medium also for non-journalists. Many online media integrate bloggers into their journalistic offerings.

Weblogs, short blogs
(the word is actually a neuter, but increasingly also masculine), are a further development of the diary under a web interface. The main characteristic is the chronological order: the latest is at the top.

The single entry *(entry)* often consists of an opinionated teaser. It links to interesting sites on the web – often to other weblogs. Sometimes, however, the entry is simply text in the blog. Since each entry has its own *URL* (web address), entries often link to texts in other blogs as well.

To find out who links to an entry in your own blog, the *trackback* is helpful. The *bloggers* (blog participants) involved exchange so-called *pings (technical queries as to how the other can be reached)* in order to be able to identify each other. The trackback in the follow-up entry ensures an automatic notification of the author who is referred to.

There are blogs that are run by a single person and those that allow all members of the community to contribute content. The form combines the possibility of communication that a forum provides with hypertext.

A diary with links, photos, audio and video elements and direct response option – the blogs have emerged from this. The *comments* (answers) are usually opinionated. The entries are written by the respective operator of the blog. Because of their high identity-forming function, blogs are often used to form a community.

Technically, blogs are easy to implement since there is standard software from manufacturers such as blogger.com or Wordpress (wordpress.com as a platform, wordpress.org as software). With a few mouse clicks, a blog is founded.

Via weblog, users also share their link collection with each other.

Audio clips and videos can be shared via podcast. The term is a combination of "iPod" (MP3 player) and "broadcasting". Audio recordings (self-made radio shows or music) are exchanged, which users can download as MP3 files to listen to on their PC or mobile device.

All weblog services can be subscribed to via RSS feed (special data format that manages text independently of its presentation), which means: With the help of a special RSS reader, you are automatically informed when something new has been published.

Twitter originated as a *microblogging service,* but has developed into a complete social media platform. As Twitter became formative for many other social media platforms, it gets its own brief here. Short status messages similar to a text message are exchanged via the Twitter platform online. Content from blogs and other websites can be quickly disseminated through Twitter posts. The shortened web address (tiny URL) is used for this purpose. The activity of writing on Twitter is colloquially referred to as "tweeting".

The posts on Twitter are called *"tweets".* The community is based on subscribing to messages from other users. The aim is to get as many subscribers or "followers" as possible for one's own entries. The posts of the people you follow are displayed in a timeline controlled by an algorithm.

Users registered with the platform can enter their own text messages with a maximum of 280 characters and send them to other users. Entire stories are distributed as threads and announced in the first tweet. Most of the time, people write in the first person. Comments by readers on a post are possible.

The term hashtag originally comes from Twitter, example: "#hashtag". Hashtags are inserted directly into the actual message; every word preceded by a hash mark is interpreted as a *tag.* Well-chosen hashtags are essential for finding a message on Twitter or Instagram.

Journalists use Twitter for research on the one hand. However, this does not work purely receptively. If you want to profit from the Twitter community, you have to actively tweet yourself. But to regard Twitter as a pure broadcasting medium is also a misunderstanding: Like all communication-oriented communities, Twitter thrives on the exchange between users. Municipalities therefore offer Twitter feeds on their current projects and discuss with citizens via Twitter and blog, universities distribute information to their students and use Twitter for teaching evaluation. Online newsrooms use Twitter to disseminate news and information about new posts and to communicate with their audience. Micro-blogging functions as a marketing and market research tool.

Via a programming interface (API), the messages published via Twitter are available to other services, so that the updates can be retrieved on various channels and also fed into the service from there.

Forums or groups are also something like the ancestor of online communication. They go back to a classic Internet service invented by students. In order to save transmission time and costs, they did not want to read the messages online, but rather transfer them collectively to their home PC during a short online contact.

Store-and-forward was the principle. In countries with high communication costs or poor online connections, e-mail is sometimes still transmitted according to this collect-and-collect scheme. The saving is an online connection that is kept as short as possible: As soon as the prepared data packet has been transmitted, the connection is cut. Of course, messages can be transmitted in both directions: from server to user as well as from user to server.

From a given list of topics the news are subscribed to, new news are automatically delivered to the user, sorted by topic. "News", sorted into "newsgroups", is the name of this Internet service. It is based on the ***netnews transfer protocol*** (nntp); a so-called newsreader is required to use the service. However, its use has declined sharply in the last 20 years. Today, discussion forums are almost exclusively offered via a web interface, i.e. users can simply join in the discussion via a browser.

Like a red thread, a message drags all replies behind it. "Thread" is the name of such a discussion context, whose visualization is reminiscent of a folder system. The individual messages themselves look like public e-mails: with sender information, subject and text. Some news programs visualize these links accordingly:

Online discussions quickly get out of hand. From the forums comes the term of *flame wars,* from Wikipedia the *edit war* about the accurate representation of a fact in collaborative writing. In German-language social media platforms, one speaks with the wrong Anglicism of the *Shitstorm.* In contrast, however, there is also the *candystorm.* No matter what you get into: End it as soon as possible – with a correction, an apology, an explanation, an amendment, as the case may be.

Spam is one of the main problems of open newsgroups, along with *flame wars.* From a Monty Python movie comes the repetition of a word ad nauseam, in this case the term for a special kind of canned meat, precisely "spam". In spamming, a usually commercial advertiser sends its messages to as many blogs or forums as possible. Filter programs that work according to mathematical algorithms help to stem the flood of spam.

Do not feed the troll. Users who deliberately provoke in a forum and distract from the topic are called *trolls*. The term probably does not come from mythology, but from English fishing with a trolling line (trolling). Since troll actions are often targeted campaigns, one speaks metaphorically of "troll factories".

Against strategically deployed fake news, online editorial departments defend themselves with verification officers and entire platforms, from "fact finders" to "fact foxes". To uncover targeted strategic misinformation, enlist the help of professional researchers. Online services such as http://www.hoax-info.de or http://www.mimikama.at help to uncover misinformation or targeted falsifications.

Make the troll action transparent to your audience, and get support. If the attacks become very personal, contact the legal department of your editorial office or the legal protection insurance of your journalists' union and get support for legal action.

Editing and moderation are particularly advisable for discussion forums within the framework of online magazines. Otherwise, the danger is quite high that a well-intentioned open offer will provide a playground for advertisers and propagandists of all kinds. A well-maintained community is characterised by a high level of commitment on the part of its users – who ideally ensure that a user does not send advertising or troll messages too often.

Technical and content moderation are strongly recommended for all communities. Depending on the target group, it is sufficient to check what is happening online several times a day at regular intervals.

Turn off anonymity: User registration with password assignment is a simple way of control. Even if participation is free of charge, the mere fact that at least the operator of the website is aware of the personal data has a certain disciplining effect.

Observe legal position. Unlike e-mails and mailing lists, guest books and forums are forms of publication to which media law applies, see chapter *Law*. Since website operators are responsible for the content of online publications as soon as they become aware of them, messages that are at least relevant under criminal law must be excluded through editorial control (Fig. 6.4).

Forum moderators should convince through neutrality and competence and be able to balance between the fronts. They must be able to answer difficult individual queries by e-mail, put users who go verbally over the top in their place, and mitigate or stop discussions that get out of hand. Moderators who take extreme positions are not very convincing.

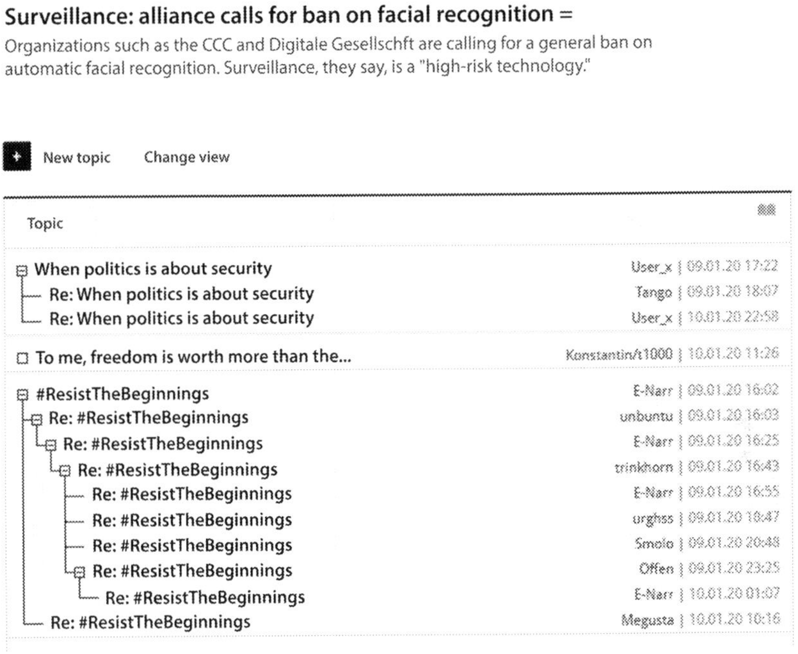

Surveillance: alliance calls for ban on facial recognition =

Organizations such as the CCC and Digitale Gesellschft are calling for a general ban on automatic facial recognition. Surveillance, they say, is a "high-risk technology."

+ New topic   Change view

Topic	
⊟ When politics is about security	User_x | 09.01.20 17:22
└─ Re: When politics is about security	Tango | 09.01.20 18:07
└─ Re: When politics is about security	User_x | 10.01.20 22:58
☐ To me, freedom is worth more than the...	Konstantin/t1000 | 10.01.20 11:26
⊟ #ResistTheBeginnings	E-Narr | 09.01.20 16:02
└⊟ Re: #ResistTheBeginnings	unbuntu | 09.01.20 16:03
└⊟ Re: #ResistTheBeginnings	E-Narr | 09.01.20 16:25
└⊟ Re: #ResistTheBeginnings	trinkhorn | 09.01.20 16:43
└─ Re: #ResistTheBeginnings	E-Narr | 09.01.20 16:55
└─ Re: #ResistTheBeginnings	urghss | 09.01.20 18:47
└─ Re: #ResistTheBeginnings	Smolo | 09.01.20 20:48
└⊟ Re: #ResistTheBeginnings	Offen | 09.01.20 23:25
└─ Re: #ResistTheBeginnings	E-Narr | 10.01.20 01:07
└─ Re: #ResistTheBeginnings	Megusta | 10.01.20 10:16

Fig. 6.4 Golem (On Golem, there is a discussion forum for each contribution. The folder structure of the threads is clearly visible)

A netiquette published online can have a disciplining effect on the users if the moderation additionally presses for their compliance. Unlocking the forums significantly increases their acceptance among users. Conversely, users appreciate the quality of the contributions in an editorially edited online magazine. As with mailing lists, simple measures such as requiring users to register (free of charge), separating the lists according to target groups, such as "patients" and "experts", and rating systems can help.

To ensure that the forums are visited by the users, write moderator or editor teasers for the corresponding entries of the online magazine. Within the forum, it is part of their job to find topics, to focus them on one or more central questions and either to write an initial text themselves or to find and brief an author for it. All these activities are part of the job description of the online editor.

6.5   Community Building

For a functioning participatory online offering, a community that follows and supports the offering on all channels is essential.

The characteristics of a community are:

1. a group of registered users
2. often specialization in a particular subject
3. integration of content and communication.

Communities usually offer the following functions to their users:

- *Collaborative creation* and linking of cross-media content (text, image, audio, video).
- *Personal profile* with settings regarding visibility to members of the network community or the public in general.
- *Contact list* or *address book,* including functions to manage referrals to these other members of the network community (such as friends, acquaintances, colleagues, etc.).
- *Tiered messages* to groups of members (individual, close friends, friends, everyone, etc.).
- *Notifications about various events* (profile changes, posted pictures, videos, reviews, call waiting, etc.).
- Collective *evaluation* of contents or also persons.

Special Interest Communities are aimed at user groups with the same *thematic* interests, for example sailors or railway enthusiasts. The more the community is anchored in the respective scene, the better for the community building. Communities for special *target groups,* for example doctors or lawyers, often suffer from the fact that the common interests of these target groups remain diffuse. *Public interest communities* deal with general topics such as fitness or eroticism – they should at least differentiate according to age groups. Here, the task of bundling the common interest of the users and binding users to the community is particularly difficult.

Also online games and video games are mostly designed as virtual worlds. The spectrum ranges from interactive games (users play with the program) to participatory worlds of experience in which the user can control game characters (avatars) and make contact with other users. Online they have a firm place in infotainment and edutainment as well as in marketing. Among other things, they are used as sweepstakes to acquire new customer addresses.

A mother medium often contributes significantly to the creation of a community's identity. For example, one of the first communities, "The Well", which Howard Rheingold describes, was created in the environment of a printed catalogue. The Tatort community, neon.de for the magazine Neon or jetzt.de, the community for the youth magazine of the Süddeutsche Zeitung, whose print edition was discontinued, are legendary examples of communities for television shows and magazines. Separate communities were created for friends of radio plays or certain radio stations. Partial communities on Instagram or Xing have become an integral part of most people's private and professional lives.

How do you build a community? According to marketing experts Hagel and Armstrong, four steps lead to success: The community wins new customers almost by itself through attractive content and corresponding advertising. The members are actively involved in the "community" – ideally by creating their own content in forums. This creates loyalty and brand loyalty. Thus, all parties involved have achieved added value – a win–win situation. Hagel and Armstrong describe the stages as follows:

1. **Build up a member base.** This requires high-quality and well-prepared content that is accessible to users free of charge. The development is accompanied by appropriate marketing activities to introduce the community to the target group.
2. **Encourage participation.** To encourage active participation in the community, users are encouraged to contribute their own content. Bringing in renowned experts increases the attractiveness.
3. **Build loyalty.** Targeted moderation and the operator's own commitment promote the development of personal relationships between users. This includes that the users start to visit the community regularly.
4. **Start business use.** According to Hagel and Armstrong, the operator can now start generating revenue through advertising, charging participation fees. Special services and linking with e-commerce platforms (marketplaces, shops or malls) are the final step.

Amitai Etzioni understands something quite different among communities. For him, five factors make up an online community:

1. a network of cordial relations,
2. a simple and open access,
3. getting to know and understand each other,
4. dialogue and feedback, and
5. a common memory, a shared history. (Interview for the online magazine Telepolis at http://www.heise.de)

This comes close to the ideas of Howard Rheingold, who was the first to speak of "virtual communities". He made the group around The Well famous in the 1980s: artists, journalists, preachers of an alternative life in the middle of California.

Requirements for a community,
accepted by the users are

- a coherent concept,
- cooperation with the right partners and
- permanent professional editing and moderation.

Your online offering will be most coherent if you plan it as a community from the outset. This means that you plan a discussion forum for every channel that makes sense. For chats, set up a time slot in which such events take place regularly. Plan possible chats, their participants and the advertising for them and coordinate the dates with your parent medium.

Corporate identity and corporate design should be maintained across all areas of your online offering: from hypertext to e-mail with users, chat and discussion forums. If there is a parent medium, its brand character has an effect across all areas of the community – i.e. also in the multimedia and participative forms: Moderation, language and style in the expert chat of the subscription daily newspaper follow different guidelines than in the celebrity chat of the music station. Conversely, the comments have an effect on the brand of the parent medium. This means: appropriate training of the online editorial team.

Finding topics for chat and forums is one of the main journalistic tasks and follows the overall concept of the online magazine, as well as writing teasers for all areas of the community.

Multiple communication options are offered to the users of a community: entering into direct dialogue with a specific user, a message to the entire group of recipients, networking with users with similar interests, a self-presentation, own blogs.

Online communities are social networks. It is easily forgotten that collaborative publishing constitutes social groups with all conceivable group problems. If you take a look at *Wikipedia*'s discussion pages, you will get a first impression of this, especially when it comes to controversial topics. Sometimes people fight for being right with a doggedness that is no longer objectively justified. Others multiply their identity and appear under several names in order to make their opinion heard. Wikipedia calls these unwanted virtual doppelgangers, behind which professional opinion makers occasionally hide, "sock puppets".

With rules of their own making, communities are trying to cope with such excesses. Local regulars' tables – real ones, not virtual ones – as well as topic-oriented meetings, trust networks and similar tools are intended to improve the communication climate.

Me-too, status fights and courtship behaviour are further effects within communities. Messages of the type 'I think so too' are meant nicely. Their information value is, apart from the relationship level, low. But the anonymous publicity of the mailing list also tempts to status fights online. One of the consequences is dachshund-like courtship and fighting behaviour.

The much-discussed hashtag #metoo for exposing sexual assault bitingly ironically cites this attitude.

Flames are the names of the notoriously sharp, witty and malicious replies to messages in mailing lists and forums. These verbal attacks usually do not seem as original to the list participants as their author believes. As a list operator, moderator, or co-discussant, you have to keep yourself in check here – and make sure that the discussion does not degenerate into a *flame war.*

What does an online moderator do?
Three main functions can be distinguished:

1. *Initiate* a *topic,*
2. *To steer* an ongoing *discussion,*
3. *Integrate participants.* What is said here with the example of the mailing list can also be transferred to forums (newsgroups) and partly also to the chat, but also to the community as a whole.

Technically, the moderator writes e-mails or fills out input masks – this can be done just as easily from home as from the editorial office. His read and write permissions are those of a "superuser": he has more rights in the network to edit and activate than the users.

Finding topics is a question of journalistic "nose", so is catching the right moment. The online moderator gains ideas for a new topic from contributions from the community. Later, these ideas often result in contributions in various forms of presentation, perhaps an entire network dossier. The moderator's introductory contribution to the topic should get to the heart of the issue. It briefly presents the various positions and ends with a question. Already here the moderator shows that he has done his research and that he himself does not take sides – this is the basis of his authority.

The moderator must **steer the discussion** in two ways. A discussion that is about to fall asleep can perhaps be rekindled with an exciting contribution that introduces a new aspect. If a discussion is in danger of becoming overly heated, a factual summary post will help. Calls from the moderator such as 'I ask for a different discussion tone here!', on the other hand, seem rather helpless, are rejected as super-teachy and also usually remain inconsequential.

Integrating participants requires a feeling for psychological moods. Does a participant feel attacked by the others? Is a user isolated by the others and made a "scapegoat"? A skilful moderator masters the various forms of communication, praising here with a personal e-mail, correcting an exaggerated statement there with a public message, and even picking up the phone in an emergency if online communication escalates.

Only when a discussion gets completely out of hand do you resort to drastic measures such as closing the mailing list or the discussion forum.

The fever curve in communities fluctuates even more strongly than in a real regulars' table discussion: Once a controversial topic has been opened, everyone can give their opinion on it in the sense of me-too – and that can quickly increase exponentially with thousands of users. Weak consolation: just as quickly as it has appeared, a topic also disappears again and is replaced by another.

In all participatory forms depending on the target group, peaks and troughs can be identified in the course of the day, week and year: afternoons (for young people), evenings and weekends (for private individuals), the summer slump, etc.

The moderation of a community is especially advisable for online magazines – a full-time job that can be grueling 24 hours a day. For busy communities, a *moderator team* is recommended: two to three people who can take turns and pass the balls to each other. It is ideal if you can recruit volunteers for the job, for whom there are gimmicks – a free subscription to the mother magazine or a small honorarium.

Technical aids in moderation start with simple filtering programs that weed out unwanted links, for example. A stop-word list that prevents four-letter words and other relevant terms helps a little to prevent the discussion from slipping. Transparency is the top priority with all these tools: users should always be informed about the rules according to which messages are filtered.

Complaint management and moderation are among the main tasks of online editors or community managers. Controlling an online discussion requires tact, but also a firm grip, because disturbances and provocations can occur, especially in *public communities*. A simple tool is the *bad list* of undesirable words: Words like Hitler or four-letter words can be excluded by software.

E-learning communities not only include audio and video sequences, but also offer platforms for learners to exchange information with each other. Learning communities are intended to ensure that the online-typical non-commitment of self-learning offers is undermined.

Further Reading

1. Bernd Oswald: Digitaler Journalismus. Zürich: Midas 2019
2. Stefan Primbs: Social Media für Journalisten (Journalistische Praxis). Wiesbaden: Springer VS 2016
3. Jan-Hinrik Schmid: Social Media. 2. Auflage. Wiesbaden: Springer VS 2018
4. Jakob Vicari: Journalismus der Dinge. Strategien für den Journalismus 4.0, Köln: Herbert von Halem 2019

The Right

7

Abstract

This is about legal issues relevant to online media in German law: The first article provides an overview of the basics, responsibility for online content and linking. The second article is dedicated to copyright and exploitation, and the third to personality and likeness rights. The fourth article deals with data protection issues.

This article was written together with Marc Liesching.

The online world reflects all legally relevant activities of people: here contacts are made, business is transacted, people look for jobs, travel or quarrel and insult each other, others demonstrate; between all this, journalistic offerings mediate in text, audio and video. In many cases, therefore, the same laws apply online as elsewhere in life. Media law has not been completely reinvented for online publications either: It covers criminal and civil law issues, topics of copyright, personality and image law and data protection, contract, name and trademark law, as well as the question of freedom of the press per se. But there are now laws of their own, such as the Telemedia Act, which specifically regulates media law online, or the Interstate Media Treaty, which replaces the Interstate Broadcasting Treaty.

This chapter deals with legal issues that are relevant for online media in German law: The first article provides an overview of the basics, responsibility for online content and linking. The second article is dedicated to copyright and exploitation, and the third to personality and likeness rights. The fourth article deals with data protection issues.

© Springer Fachmedien Wiesbaden GmbH, part of Springer Nature 2022   149
G. Hooffacker, *Online journalism*,
https://doi.org/10.1007/978-3-658-35731-3_7

We have tried to present the basic regulations in an understandable way. For your online media offer, please be sure to seek legal advice. Some links to legal texts and current case law can be found at http://www.onlinejournalismus.org.

7.1   Fundamentals and Responsibility

The Internet is not a medium, but a communication channel through which various services run, including explicitly so-called online media. It has never been a "lawless space", as one sometimes reads. However, deficits often arise in law enforcement due to the anonymity and global reach of the Internet.

For journalistic activity online, the freedom of opinion guaranteed in Article 5, Paragraph 1 of the Basic Law applies as it does to all citizens: "Everyone has the right to express and disseminate his or her opinion freely in speech, writing and pictures and to inform himself or herself unhindered from generally accessible sources". In addition, special media freedoms are constitutionally guaranteed: "Freedom of the press and freedom of reporting by radio and film are guaranteed. There shall be no censorship." (Art. 5 para. 1 GG). If the Internet does not find an explicit mention, they nevertheless participate in the scope of protection of the fundamental right. This applies above all to journalistic online products, as they are always "similar to the press" or "similar to broadcasting".

The Basic Law already restricts this freedom. Article 5(2) states: "These rights shall be limited by the provisions of general law, by the laws for the protection of minors and by the right to personal honour". The legislator has made extensive and varied use of such restrictions, especially in the media sector.

Criminal liability of acts: Crimes can be committed online just as they can offline, in real life. For example, anyone who distributes stolen goods via messages in public discussion forums is liable to prosecution. The same applies to calls for criminal acts or violations of applicable laws. Often, even stricter regulations apply on the Internet, for example for social networks such as Facebook, YouTube or Twitter. These are obliged by the Network Enforcement Act (Netzwerkdurchsetzungsgesetz, NetzDG) to immediately delete certain punishable online content if they become aware of this via a complaint.

The legal basis for online journalism in Germany has been the Telemedia Act (Telemediengesetz, TMG) since March 1, 2007 and the State Treaty on Broadcasting and Telemedia (Rundfunkstaatsvertrag, RStV), which has been amended again and again since the 1990s. The latter will be replaced by the new State Media Treaty in the course of 2020. The TMG replaced the predecessor laws, the *Teleservices Act* and the *Media Services State Treaty,* and thus also the historical distinction between *teleservices* (individual communication) and *media services* (based on the classic mass media). It takes account of the structure of online offerings, which frequently offer both types of services in combination.

The State Treaty on the Media is expected to enter into force in the course of 2020. Among other things, it introduces the term "media intermediaries". This refers to social media platforms such as Google and Facebook. The regulations of the interstate treaty will also be mandatory for voice assistants such as "Alexa" in the future. They will then have to be transparent about the criteria they use to select and present content, and they will have to ensure that journalistic and editorial content can be found on an equal footing. Current information is available at http://www.onlinejournalismus.org.

The protection of minors from harmful media in German law is regulated in the "State Treaty on the Protection of Human Dignity and the Protection of Minors in Broadcasting and Telemedia" (State Treaty on the Protection of Minors in the Media (Jugendmedienschutz-Staatsvertrag, JMStV for short). The JMStV combines private broadcasting (television and radio) and telemedia (primarily the Internet) under the supervisory umbrella of the Commission for the Protection of Minors in the Media (Kommission für Jugendmedienschutz, KJM). The KJM examines whether violations of the JMStV have occurred and decides on the measures to be taken against the media provider. However, the KJM sees itself not only as a supervisory body, but also wants to initiate socio-political processes, it writes on its website (http://www.kjm-online.de/). As a subordinate body of the KJM, the organisationjugendschutz.net is active in practice, which also proactively checks online content for compliance with youth protection regulations and, if necessary, contacts the provider.

What does due diligence mean for journalistic-editorial content? Telemedia that reproduce journalistic-editorial content of periodical print products in text or image must follow the recognised journalistic principles. News must be checked for truth and origin by the provider "prior to their dissemination with the due diligence required by the circumstances". In addition, according to § 19 of the State Media Treaty, most journalistically-editorially designed online offerings must comply with the recognised journalistic principles. This applies above all to "journalistically-editorially designed telemedia offered on a business basis, which regularly contain news or political information". News must be checked for content, origin and truth by the provider prior to its dissemination with the due diligence required by the circumstances. The regulations correspond in many respects to the requirements of (state) press law, as further specified in the Press Code of the German Press Council. Accordingly, this code also applies to journalistic online products. Its guidelines can be found at http://www.presserat.info, explained with reference to current disputes.

The separation of editorial part and advertising is one of the basic rules of journalism. If a link from an editorial offer leads to a company site, this must be announced to the user in advance. The Berlin Regional Court upheld the action for an injunction brought by the Federation of German Consumer Organisations against the Bild.t-Online.de website operated by Axel Springer. The website contained an article on a car with links to sub-pages, which, in the opinion of the consumer protection agency, could be classified as advertising, but which only partially contained the reference "advertisement". Advertising links must therefore be marked as such. The State Treaty on the Media lays down rules on advertising, surreptitious advertising and sponsoring. Further advertising restrictions may result from special laws, for example in gambling or youth protection law. Furthermore, the advertising restrictions of competition law (UWG) must also be observed.

Is there a right of reply? Just as in the press sector, the right of reply for online media is regulated in state law, namely also in the State Media Treaty (§ 20)....
According to this, providers of telemedia with journalistic-editorial offers are obliged to "immediately include a counterstatement of the person or body affected by a factual allegation made in their offer in their offer without costs for the person concerned and without additional retrieval fee". The counterstatement is to be offered without insertions and omissions in the same presentation as the factual allegation.

Who is responsible for the content offered online? The TMG initially regulates the issues of responsibility and the labelling obligation. It distinguishes between content providers, access providers and host providers. And states quite clearly: The content provider is always liable for its own content. He can also be fully liable for third-party content if he has made it "his own". This is affirmed by the courts if, from the third party's point of view, the information "appears to be his own". Here, for example, the advertising behaviour of the service provider is also included in the considerations. If advertising revenue is generated for the provision of third-party content, this can already constitute an attribution of ownership with the consequence of full liability.

Those who do not offer their own content, but provides third-party content for use as a so-called host provider, i.e. operates a forum, for example, graduated rules of responsibility apply. In this case, the host provider is only responsible for third-party content if he has gained concrete knowledge of it (e.g. through complaints) and has not immediately removed the content. For social networks, very tight deletion deadlines apply in the case of criminal content. Accordingly, Facebook,

YouTube, and Twitter must delete obviously punishable content within 24 hours. However, even ignorance does not protect host providers from warnings, insofar as these have as their object the refraining from future dissemination.

So-called access providers, who merely provide access to online content, are generally not liable at all, i.e. not even if they are aware of it. The way in which search engines can be held liable depends largely on the type of service. For search hits that are the result of algorithm-based selection, criminal liability of the search engine operator is probably always excluded. Claims for deletion of search hits by private individuals are justified in individual cases ("right to be forgotten").

A liability for interviews was also affirmed by the Hamburg Regional Court. According to this, online media bear full liability for statements made by interview partners. In practice, this would mean that all statements in the interview would have to be checked and counter-researched before publication. Thomas Hoeren, Professor of Media Law at the University of Münster, comments: "One can only hope that the higher courts will gradually bring the Hamburg Regional Court back to its senses."

Is one responsible for links? In principle, you may link to external content. So-called deep links to sub-pages are also permitted. However, links can become criminally relevant if they link to criminal content. Therefore, in their own interest, website operators should regularly check their links and link collections in order to be able to prove careful editorial action.

The term "imprint" does not exist in the TMG. The regulation for telemedia, however, is based on the imprint obligation of the state press laws and goes considerably beyond these in terms of the information obligations and the threat of punishment. Section 5 (1) TMG imposes extensive "general information duties" on the operator of a business website, which he must publish on his website:

- Company name, legal form and address
- Names of the authorized representatives
- Telephone, fax, e-mail address
- Information on the competent supervisory authorities/(if any)
- Commercial, association, partnership or cooperative register including register number (if available)
- For certain professions, indication of the chamber and legal job title
- The sales tax identification number (if available)

These information requirements apply not only for websites, but also for newsletters, blogs, social media platforms and email communication. The information details must be "easily recognisable, directly accessible and permanently available" (TMG, Section 5). It is customary that the imprint is directly linked from all pages of the website, can be called up with a mouse click and is thus easy to find. The German TMG expressly requires this information to be provided "for business-like telemedia, which are generally offered for a fee" (TMG, Section 5). However, businesslike in legal parlance does not necessarily mean that money is charged for the offer, but only that the Internet offer in question is intended to be permanent. In addition, Section 18 of the new State Media Treaty already regulates comparable information obligations (name and address) for all providers of online content, "which does not exclusively serve personal or family purposes".

Since the TMG for a faulty imprint provides for fines of up to EUR 50,000 as an administrative offence, every website operator is well advised to include an imprint. In case of omissions, there is also the risk of being warned according to competition law regulations.

7.2   Copyright

Copyright law regulates all usage and licensing issues relating to content. As a rule, anyone who wants to use someone else's content must conclude a licence agreement, unless he or she is acting within the framework of the statutory copyright restrictions (e.g. right of quotation). The type of use and the period of time for which this right is granted are regulated by the copyright contract.

The Copyright and Related Rights Act (Urheberrecht und verwandte Schutzrechte, UrhG) protects the authors of personal intellectual creations (works), for example linguistic works, computer programs, database works as well as works of music, dance art, visual art, photographic and cinematographic works. In Germany, no special registration or application of the work is necessary in order to be recognised as an author. Whether websites are also protectable works depends on the individual case. As a rule, simple systematic designs and the structure of a homepage are not protected by copyright, whereas texts are, insofar as they exhibit a degree of creative idiosyncrasy, i.e. go beyond empty phrases such as "Welcome to my website!"

In addition to works, other performances are also protected if this is expressly regulated by law. These so-called other protectable performances include, for example, photographs or databases, which do not yet reach the required level of creation of a work. Link collections can also be protected by copyright as databases. The so-called ancillary copyright for press publishers is a much-discussed German intellectual property right that was introduced in 2013. It was intended to protect publishing services "against systematic access (...) by the providers of search engines and providers of such services on the net (...), which prepare content in accordance with a search engine (...) (and thereby) also (access) third-party publishing services for their own value creation". In 2019, the ECJ ruled that the German ancillary copyright was not applicable because the German government had not submitted the draft to the EU Commission in advance.

What copyright does not protect is the idea for a text, a book, a film. The factual content of a work is also not protected: The moment the self-researched news is online, its factual content is free. Also a certain way of presentation, a special design, are not protected. That is why good ideas, news and good design spread quickly online.

Right of attribution. According to Section 12 UrhG, every author has the (personal) right to decide on the publication of his or her work, and according to Section 13 UrhG, he or she has the right to decide whether this publication is made with or without attribution. If you are an online journalist and supply photos or graphics, you should insist on your right of attribution. This indicates their authorship and is a good advertising opportunity for their own work.

Right of exploitation and adequate remuneration. The author holds the exclusive right to exploit his work, including an "appropriate" share in the economic benefit to be derived from it. According to Sections 22–24 UrhG, this also includes modifications of the work, for which the author must give his consent. Since the copyright reform in 2002, Section 11 UrhG states: "Copyright protects the author in his intellectual and personal relationship to the work and in the use of the work. It serves at the same time to provide reasonable remuneration for the use of the work." What constitutes reasonable remuneration, the law does not specify in numbers. Instead, it provides four benchmarks for the courts to decide in the event of a dispute:

- If there are *collective agreements,* as in the case of quasi-employee freelancers at daily newspapers, the remuneration stated here is considered appropriate;
- in all other cases, the relevant associations of authors and users should establish *common remuneration rules;*
- where there is neither a collective agreement nor remuneration rules, "what is customarily and reasonably to be paid in the course of business", i.e. what is *customary in the industry* and is also fair, is deemed to be reasonable;
- where there is no agreement, a *conciliation board* is supposed to help.

For information on standard market remuneration for online journalists, see the chapter on "The profession".

The appropriate remuneration does not exist automatically. If you signed a contract that turned out to be a bad deal after the fact, you have to ask for a fee increase from the other party first. And that goes like this:

First of all, the contractually agreed fee applies. If it is not appropriate according to the above-mentioned standards, one demands an increased fee from the client. If you cannot agree on the amount of the fee, you have to file a lawsuit to change the contract (legal protection by a journalists' union is extremely helpful!). It is not the entire contract that has to be contested, but only the amount of the fee. The contract as such remains in force.

Anyone who uses works by other authors that enjoy copyright protection must generally acquire a licence to use them. As a rule, licenses for individual types of use can be acquired from the collecting societies. If this is not the case, the respective rights holder must be located and requested to grant a licence/consent to use.

Creative Commons licenses allow the use of content under certain conditions – up to unrestricted use. Behind this is a non-profit organization, founded in 2001 in the USA, which makes these standard license agreements available. Many media contents on Wikipedia can be used under such precisely defined conditions.

In many cases, however, works can be used freely. First of all, so-called official works (e.g. legal texts, reasons for judgements) can always be used freely. Works whose term of protection has expired (usually 70 years after the death of the creator) can also be freely used. The Copyright Act also regulates numerous exceptions in which copyright-protected works of others can be used without obtaining a licence. Well-known examples are private copying (Section 53 UrhG) or the right to quote (Section 51 UrhG). In the journalistic context, Section 50 UrhG is also of particular importance. For the reporting of daily events on the radio, in newspapers and magazines, the copying, distribution and communication to the public of works that become perceptible in the course of these events are permitted to the extent required by the purpose. Exceptions for press reviews and mixed news are also regulated by Section 49 UrhG. Only the copying of individual articles is permitted, but not, for example, the copying of the text of an entire issue. The extent to which this also applies to press reviews on the Internet is disputed. Thomas Hoeren says: "The problem has in fact been defused by the fact that Pressemonitor GmbH is now active together with VG Wort in the area of press review remuneration."

Sources on copyright can be found at http://www.urheberrecht.org and at http://www.onlinejournalismus.org.

Money from the collecting societies. Films can be copied onto data carriers, newspapers can be scanned and music from the radio can be stored. Since, in the age of mass copying, journalists can no longer be expected to keep track of all other uses such as photocopying or others, the collecting societies were founded. Good news: here you can get money without having to do much for it. This is especially true for journalists who write texts, take photographs or make films (for musicians, it is a bit more complicated). You only have to register; there are no membership fees to pay.

The collecting society Wort (VG Wort) is a must for everyone who writes professionally, whether on a permanent basis or freelance, whether for the press, radio or the Internet. The VG Wort collects the money from the exploiters and distributes it to the authors. Anyone who manufactures or imports devices that can be used to copy copyrighted works must pay so-called "device levies". From each device sold, royalties go to the collecting society. The society distributes the money to the authors. Reading circles, press reviews, libraries and school book publishers also pay the VG Wort for these second uses. Authors and journalists are then paid according to fixed rules for publications on the Internet, in the press and on radio and television, as well as for academic publications. The condition is that one concludes a free of charge management contract with the VG Wort. Not only freelancers but also employed journalists can report their publications within a certain period of time, usually simply using an online form. The procedure for digitised texts and texts published online is somewhat more complicated and is described at http://www.vgwort.de.

The collecting society Bild-Kunst (VG Bild-Kunst) is the right address for photojournalists. Its task is to protect the exploitation rights of image authors from different media; in addition, it maintains a *social welfare organisation* for members in financial need from its income. *Professional group II* is relevant for photojournalists. Since the distribution of library and photocopy fees alone can amount to several hundred euros a year, every photojournalist should be a member of VG Bild-Kunst. Membership is free of charge (in analogy to the VG Wort's rights management contract) and is a prerequisite for being able to assert one's claims. VG Bild-Kunst also grants its members legal protection to a limited extent. (http://www.bildkunst.de).

Multimedia content. The best known is the Society for Musical Performing and Mechanical Reproduction Rights (Gesellschaft für musikalische Aufführungs- und mechanische Vervielfältigungsrechte, GEMA), which is active in the field of *music rights*. However, it can be expensive to register as an author of musical works of art. Therefore, you should inform yourself in detail beforehand (http://www.gema.de). Membership in GEMA is voluntary. Authors are free to exercise their rights themselves or to assign them to GEMA. In order to be represented by GEMA, authors, i.e. composers and lyricists or their publishers, must become members. Anyone who registers must register all his or her works with GEMA from that point on. Users of these works, producers of (visual) sound carriers, radio and television broadcasters, organisers of live music and operators of Internet offerings acquire from GEMA the rights to use a royalty, which is distributed to the rightholders after deduction of an administrative fee.

Who makes movies can turn to the collecting society for rights of use an Filmwerke (Verwertungsgesellschaft für Nutzungsrechte an Filmwerken mbH, VGF). The VGF administers the rights of German and foreign film producers and directors of feature films (http://www.vgf.de). In addition, there is the collecting society for film and television producers (Verwertungsgesellschaft der Film- und Fernsehproduzenten mbH, VFF). One can assign the rights to films and motion pictures to the VFF as a trustee for the territory of the Federal Republic of Germany (http://www.vffvg.de). In some cases, the VG Bild-Kunst is responsible (http://www.bildkunst.de), sometimes also the GÜFA or the GWFF (http://www.guefa.de, http://www.gwff.de).

Simple and exclusive rights of use. Publications in daily newspapers fall under the *simple right of use,* unless otherwise contractually agreed. "Whoever grants the online newspaper a simple right of use to an article may even sell the same article to the competing medium days before in a version with the same wording." (Götz Buchholz). If the client wants exclusivity, he must contractually agree on it as an *exclusive right of use* – and usually pay a little more for it.

In author contracts, it is common to grant the client the right to transfer rights of use to third parties – who then take care of translating the text into other languages, for example. The author receives the contractually agreed shares.

Under no circumstances may you simply reproduce photos or even comics online on your own pages if you have not clarified the licenses. In addition to the copyrights, which in the case of Donald Duck, for example, are held by Walt Disney Corp. in the USA, such comics are also additionally protected trademarks. The characters are commercially exploited by the rights holders, whether for chewing gum advertising or as T-shirt imprints. Such rights must first be acquired from the rights holders; a license fee is then paid to the rights holder for each T-shirt sold with a Donald Duck print.

7.3   Right of Personality and Likeness

In recent decades, the Federal Constitutional Court has drawn a broad scope of protection, especially in the area of the media, for persons who are reported on in words and images in journalistic products. This concerns, on the one hand, statements about these persons (right of expression) and, on the other hand, depictions of images (right to one's own image).

If untruthful facts are claimed in online content with regard to a person, this generally constitutes a violation of personal rights, against which the person concerned can take legal action. In addition to the aforementioned counterstatement claim (Section 20 of the State Media Treaty), a civil law claim for deletion and injunctive relief and, in extreme cases, even damages can be considered.

However, the personal rights of journalists must also be respected when they make assessments about people. If the criticism is unobjective or even an insult, the statement can also be prohibited. In all cases, the criminal law on insults applies. In the context of reporting on suspicions, restrictions due to the personal rights of the persons concerned must also be accepted. In this case, the type of reporting (e.g. use of secretly made recordings) must always be weighed against the interest in reporting and the protection of personality rights. Furthermore, the criminal law on insults also covers defamation and so-called "slander" (§§ 185–187 StGB).

Right to one's own image. As a rule, anyone who acts without the consent of the persons recorded is already acting unlawfully when filming or photographing. Anyone who captures and reproduces people in photos, audio or video works must also observe the rights to the protection of personality. In the case of children and young people under the age of 18, it is essential to obtain the consent of their parents. Example: If a video is to be shot at the school festival, this parental consent can be obtained by means of a form.

Employees of a company may also only be depicted on the Internet with their consent. Consent to use a photograph for personnel purposes does not automatically extend to the Internet.

Unauthorised sound and image recordings can also be punishable. According to Section 201 of the Criminal Code, it is prohibited to record the non-public spoken word of another person on a sound recording medium. In addition, it is not permitted to record images of persons in their most personal sphere of life, e.g. in their home or in a room that is particularly protected against viewing (Section 201a StGB). This so-called "paparazzi" paragraph has already been tightened up several times by the legislator and now also includes the taking of pictures that show the helplessness of another person.

7.4   Data Protection

Who wants their own usage data to be analysed by private or state agencies – for economic or political purposes? At the European level, a regulation, the GDPR, regulates data protection in all European member states (https://eur-lex.europa.eu/legal-content/DE/TXT/PDF/?uri=OJ:L:2016:119:FULL&from=EN). The aim is to protect the privacy of users in the case of Big Data, web tracking and profiling and to provide a "right to be forgotten". The European Data Protection Regulation has increased the transparency obligations of companies towards their customers. Data subjects should know what happens to their data and for what purposes the data is processed.

A lot of **usage data** are technically necessary for the functioning of a website. This must be explained to the users. Other data may also be stored and processed, you just have to tell them how, for how long and according to which rules they are stored. So you can collect, store and analyse data, but you have to communicate it on an accessible page and the users have to agree to it.

According to TMG, users of telemedia must already be informed "at the beginning of the usage process" "in a generally understandable form" "about the type, scope and purpose of the collection and use of personal data". If applicable, you must inform users that they can object to the creation of pseudonymous usage profiles (web tracking). In addition, you must point out the possibility of using the online offer anonymously or under a pseudonym.

Under data protection law, third-party platforms such as Facebook or TikTok are questionable, because you as a provider have no way of influencing the type, scope and evaluation of the stored data. You can only refer to the operators of these platforms. The European Court of Justice (judgment of 05 June 2018 – C-210/16) has ruled that in a particular case, the operator of Facebook fanpages is also responsible for data processing in addition to Facebook. What this means for media offerings on Facebook has yet to be explored.

The GDPR has some positive consequences for consumers, writes the data protection organization Digitalcourage on its website. Among others are anchored.

- Right to a privacy-friendly service – In future, the right to data portability and data protection by design and by default will help to achieve this.
- Data minimisation and prohibition of tying – The principle of data minimisation is implemented, the prohibition of tying is indirectly included in Article 7.
- Data may only be used for the purposes for which they were collected. – Purpose limitation is included in a compromise.
- Citizens must explicitly consent to the processing of their data. – Instead of explicit consent, clear consent is included.

Research (private market research) must not become a backdoor for companies to use personal data arbitrarily and without the consent of the data subjects. – Research is limited in Article 83 to research in the public interest, history, science and statistics. (https://digitalcourage.de/blog/2015/geschafft-neuer-datenschutz-fuer-die-europaeische-union, retrieved 9 January 2020).

Anyone who runs a blog or website must observe what applies to all website operators (this is not covered by the so-called media privilege, which contains special regulations for journalistic-editorial products).

In these areas, citizens have, for example, the right to obtain information about their data. Websites must also comply with the obligation to minimise data, transmit data from contact forms in encrypted form and observe other technical security precautions. In particular, website operators are obliged to provide a legally compliant privacy policy. Those who already have one must adapt it.

If the data privacy statement is missing on a website, this constitutes an infringement of competition law that can be claimed against. You can find some "data protection notice generators" online that provide useful results. A good checklist of what to pay attention to is provided by the Webpunks on their website:

DSGVO checklist

- Imprint and privacy policy on the website
- Use of Google Analytics
- Use of cookies
- Opt-out of data collection and deletion and rectification of stored data
- Newsletter, especially third-party providers such as Mailchimp
- Contact forms
- Images and data of employees on the website
- Share buttons
- Comment function for pages and blog posts
- User registration

Read more at https://www.webpunks.co/dsgvo-und-webseiten/#impressum-datenschutz, retrieved January 9, 2020.

Anyone who uses publicly available electronic communications services or operates a public communications network is obliged to make certain data available to government agencies. This is justified with an improved possibility to prevent or avoid criminal offences. This so-called *data retention* (VDS) obliges to store the data of all contractual partners "in advance".

Further Reading

1. Udo Branahl, Medienrecht. Eine Einführung, Wiesbaden: Springer VS (2013)
2. Fechner/Mayer (Hrsg.). Medienrecht – Vorschriftensammlung, Heidelberg: C.F. Müller, 15. Aufl. 2019 (jährlich aktualisiert)
3. Thomas Hoeren, Grundzüge des Internetrechts. München: C. H. Beck 2017 sowie laufend aktualisiert   online: https://www.itm.nrw/wp-content/uploads/Skript-Internetrecht-Maerz-2018.pdf
4. Paschke/Berlit / Meyer (Hrsg.), Hamburger Kommentar Gesamtes Medienrecht, Baden-Baden: Nomos, 4. Auflage 2020
5. TMG: http://www.gesetze-im-internet.de/tmg/
6. Medienstaatsvertrag: https://www.rlp.de/fileadmin/rlp-stk/pdf-Dateien/Medienpolitik/ModStV_MStV_und_JMStV_2019-12-05_MPK.pdf

Further Links

7. https://digitalcourage.de
8. https://dsgvo-gesetz.de/
9. https://irights.info (dort auch viele nützliche Publikationen zum Download)
10. https://www.urheberrecht.org
11. https://www.mediafon.net

Education and Training

8

Abstract

Journalistic, technical and organisational skills that online journalists need are acquired throughout one's life – by practising the profession.

But how to start? And what to choose: the 2-day course "Shooting with the smartphone" or the master's degree course? Those who are just graduating from school tend to look for *training opportunities,* while those who are already in a (media) profession want to *continue* their education. This chapter provides tips.

The overview of the training opportunities

- We start with *courses of study at universities and universities of applied sciences.*
- All major *journalism schools* have integrated online modules and cross-media work into their teaching.
- With its practical relevance, the *traineeship* is an excellent basis for a career in online journalism.
- Today, the *vocational further training courses* offered by the vocational academies, which usually last *1 year,* generally require a degree.
- Some training courses are also available on a *part-time basis,* including some as *distance learning courses (e-learning).*
- *Short courses lasting several days* are primarily intended for journalists who are already working and who wish to develop their skills in one or other specialist area.
- *Networks and contact exchanges* are needed by online journalists at the beginning of their career to gain a foothold, but also to stay in business. At the end of the chapter, you will read about different ways to make such contacts.

© Springer Fachmedien Wiesbaden GmbH, part of Springer Nature 2022   163
G. Hooffacker, *Online journalism,*
https://doi.org/10.1007/978-3-658-35731-3_8

The overview in the book is up to date as of January 2020 and treats institutions in Germany, Austria and Switzerland. We have compiled up-to-date information including hyperlinks for you at http://www.onlinejournalismus.org. Is your offer missing? Then please send an e-mail to gabriele@hooffacker.de – we update the online pages for the book regularly.

8.1   Universities

A-levels – then what? A specialized degree is still a solid basis for an online journalistic job. These and many other ways into journalism in general can be found in the textbook "Introduction to Practical Journalism (Einführung in den praktischen Journalismus)" by Walther von La Roche. Therefore, we have refrained from providing general information on this in the following.

In this section, only universities of applied sciences and universities are mentioned that explicitly offer study programmes for online journalism.

More and more courses of study are aimed at future online journalists:

Germany's first online journalism course at Darmstadt University of Applied Sciences has now become a seven-semester Bachelor's degree program. It is part of the Media Department at Darmstadt University of Applied Sciences (http://www.h-da.de), which is located on the Dieburg campus. It started in 2001 with 40 students. The course starts with basic training; students can then specialise in online journalism or online PR.

The bachelor's degree program in Online Editing has been offered by *TH Köln* (http://www.th-koeln.de) since the summer semester 2019. It imparts basic knowledge of communication science, professional working techniques and department-specific factual knowledge.

A Multimedia Production degree program with Bachelor's and Master's degrees has already existed since the winter semester 1998/1999 at the *Kiel University of Applied Sciences* (http://www.fh-kiel.de).

Numerous degree courses have the word "cross-media" in their name. Editorial work is not always the focus here. Here, the focus is primarily on editing:

The "Cross-media Editing/Public Relations (CR)" course of study at the *Stuttgart Media University (Hochschule der Medien Stuttgart,* HdM) has a standard period of study of 7 semesters and ends with the degree "Bachelor of Arts" (http://www.hdm-stuttgart.de).

Technical Journalism is the name of the bachelor's degree programme at *Bonn-Rhein-Sieg University of Applied Sciences* (http://www.h-brs.de), which has been in existence for some time. The course covers topics from mechanical engineering and physics as well as journalism. Recently, the bachelor's degree course in **Visual Technical Communication** was added.

In **Nuremberg, the Technical University** Georg Simon Ohm has also been offering a bachelor's degree in technical journalism since 2009/2010 (http://www. th-nuernberg.de).

At the **University of Applied Sciences Würzburg-Schweinfurt,** you can take a four-semester master's course in technical journalism (http://www.fh-wuerzburg.de).

A **degree in media technology** (Media Engineering) brings you the necessary technical knowledge for multimodal media production. However, not all media engineering degree programmes include content-related, journalistic modules. This is the case in the Media Technology degree programme at Leipzig University of Applied Sciences (HTWK Leipzig) (http://www.htwk-leipzig.de). In individual cases, read the programme overview and the module handbook carefully!

All proven journalism courses contain online modules. Numerous online topics are hidden behind the buzzword *digital journalism.* Even within the framework of journalism or communication studies, quite a few institutes have additional online-specific seminars in their programmes. I refer to "La Roche's Introduction to Practical Journalism" or the website for the book, which lists these courses in full (http://www.praktischer-journalismus.de) (Fig. 8.1).

Fig. 8.1 Klaus Meier of the Catholic University of Eichstätt on online journalism and journalism training at universities and in journalism schools (https://www.gelbe-reihe.de/online-journalismus/prof-dr-klaus-meier-journalistenausbildung/ or directly https://youtu.be/fF-hbIhE6xI)

8.2   Journalism Schools and Traineeships

Most journalism schools are of the opinion: "The online journalist also needs the classic core competence of the journalist" (Rudolf Porsch, Axel Springer School of Journalism). That is why they have integrated online and cross-media modules into their training. However, some also organise special seminars on online journalism.

The *German School of Journalism* (http://www.djs-online.de) in Munich has integrated an "Online" course lasting several weeks into its training, as has the *Henri Nannen School* (http://www.journalistenschule.de).

The *Axel Springer Academy* in Berlin trains its journalism students as cross-media trainees: They get to create the *world* compact as well as experience cross-media training (http://www.axel-springer-akademie.de).

At the *EMS Electronic Media School/School for New Media (Schule für neue Medien)* (http://www.ems-babelsberg.de), the training lasts a total of 18 months and qualifies students for work in the electronic media of radio, television and the Internet.

The curriculum for the 2-year training course at the *RTL School of Journalism for TV and Multimedia* (http://www.rtl-journalistenschule.de) includes an intensive multimedia course.

The *Burda School of Journalism (BJS)* (http://www.burda-Journalistenschule. de) in Offenburg takes a similar approach.

Where volunteers are offered everywhere, what a volunteer earns and how to apply for a volunteer position are described in the textbook "La Roche's Introduction to Practical Journalism". For several years now, there have been dedicated *online volunteer courses. Online course modules* have now been included in the programmes of almost all educational institutions that offer *volunteer courses.*

Examples: As part of the basic courses for trainees at the *Academy of the Bavarian Press (Akademie der Bayerischen Presse, ABP),* there are separate online courses (http://www.akademie-bayerische-presse.de), as well as at the Berlin School of Journalism (Berliner Journalistenschule) (http://www.berliner-journalisten-schule.de).

8.3   Continuing Vocational Training, In-service and Distance Learning Courses

Private multimedia and journalism academies currently (as of January 2020) offer 2- to 6-month courses with a focus on online journalism. The quality of the training stands and falls with the course concept and the selection of the lecturers.

Interested parties should arrange a "taster day" to get an impression of the training and ask for references and placement rates.

The education and training on these courses must usually be paid by the students. In very many cases, further education is funded by the employment agency, the municipality or the pension insurance within the framework of the education voucher. A list of links to providers of such courses can be found on the web pages for this book.

Online Journalism is the focus of the *Academy of Journalism (Journalistenakademie),* (http://www.journalistenakademie.de), which was the first to offer this course nationwide. Here, there are courses for online editor and press officer cross-media.

Further education courses via digital platforms, without lecturers on site, are offered in various cities, for example by *WBS Training AG* (http://www.wbstraining.de) or the Cologne-based mibeg Institute (http://www.mibeg.de).

Journalistic further education in part-time or distance learning courses: This requires a high level of self-discipline from the participants. They are rewarded at the end with certificates or even a degree. Individual modules are available on-site, others exclusively as distance learning courses. If both are combined, this is called "blended learning". Instead of "distance learning" one often reads "e-learning". The methods are supplemented by individual tutoring and exchange via the learning community of the course provider.

The Reporter Factory (Reporterfabrik) aims to help qualify the public for journalism in the digital age. In doing so, it takes into account the fact that journalists and users are working ever more closely together. Both sides can benefit from the free courses offered by the Reporter Factory. The Reporter Factory is headed by Cordt Schnibben, a long-time editor at *Spiegel* and *ZEIT*; the managing directors are David Schraven and Simon Kretschmer, both at the research portal *Correctiv.* The courses on offer range from practical journalistic craft ("shooting with the smartphone") to current topics and basic media knowledge. Some of the workshops are free, others cost between 5 and 25 € (http://reporterfabrik.org).

In distance learning courses, additional qualifications (language, technology) can be acquired. They cannot replace practical journalistic experience. You should ask for references from graduates beforehand and find out what the reputation of the respective school is like.

Courses around "Creating, maintaining and controlling web content" are offered by *akademie.de* (http://www.akademie.de).

Also with the *Study Community Darmstadt (Studiengemeinschaft Darmstadt),* one can become online editor in a pure online training course (http://www.sgd.de).

Under the column "advertisement and creativity", the *distance academy for adult education (Fernakademie für Erwachsenenbildung)* offers a correspondence course to online journalists (http://www.fernakademie-klett.de).

The *Institute for Learning Systems (Institut für Lernsysteme)*, which also belongs to the Klett Group, offers such a distance learning course at the same address (http://www.ils.de).

The Free School of Journalism (Freie Journalistenschule, FJS) (http://www.freie-journalistenschule.de) has integrated an online journalism module into its distance learning course.

8.4   Short Courses

Learning the essentials of "writing for the web" in 2–5 days is possible if you do not start from scratch. Most of the 1-day or multi-day courses are therefore aimed at journalists who are already working. Those who are interested in such a course should in any case have some professional experience in publishing Internet or intranet articles. In case of doubt, it helps to ask what knowledge is required.

The two journalists' unions the German Journalists' Association (Deutscher Journalistenverband, djv) and the German Union of Journalists (Deutsche Journalistinnen- und Journalist/innen-Union, dju) offer such courses at a reasonable price for their members:

Courses lasting several days can be booked at the regional associations of the *German Journalists' Association* (http://www.djv.de), especially in Baden-Württemberg.

The *dju* offers its own seminars as well as courses with cooperation partners *in the trade union ver.di* (http://dju.verdi.de and http://www.journalistenakademie.de).

Many of the journalism education and training institutions also offer short-term courses between 2 and 5 days. These include:

Academy of Journalism, http://www.akademie-fuer-publizistik.de
Academy of the Bavarian Press (ABP), http://www.akademie-bayerische-presse.de
Academy of Journalism, http://www.journalistenakademie.de

Educational institutions of political parties and churches also often have inexpensive short courses on practical journalism in their programmes, which can be recommended in terms of quality. Examples:

The *Academy for Political Education in Tutzing* (http://www.apb-tutzing.de) regularly invites participants to seminars on media policy, but also very practical seminars on online research and online publishing.

The *Hanns Seidel Foundation*'s support programme covers all media including multimedia (maximum age: 35). The seminars, which usually last a weekend, take place in the professionally equipped educational centers Kloster Banz and Wildbad Kreuth (http://www.hss.de).

Seminars lasting several days on online research, online publishing and current topics are held throughout Germany by the *Journalists' Academy of the Friedrich Ebert Foundation*, Berlin and Bonn (http://www.fes.de).

The *Protestant Media Academy* (http://www.evangelische-medienakademie.de) offers weekend and week-long seminars on cross-media topics.

Basic courses, research and design seminars for the Internet are offered by the Catholic School of Journalism ifp (http://journalistenschule-ifp.de/).

Youth and adult education institutions often associate online journalism courses with media education objectives; they are aimed at educators and other multipliers in the education sector. Examples:

The *Remscheid Academy* organises weekly courses on multimedia and online media as well as directly on online editing (http://www.akademieremscheid.de).

It is also worth taking a look at the local adult education programme. The *Nuremberg Education Centre*, for example, always has courses on blogs, journalism and public relations in its online programme (http://bz.nuernberg.de/).

8.5   Networks and Contact Exchanges

Training on the job is still a possible way into the young profession of online journalism. Even if you do not attend any of the above-mentioned training institutions, you can become a good journalist: some tips can be found here. More links can be found at http://www.onlinejournalismus.org.

For active training on the job, we distinguish three possibilities:

1. Membership in one of the *networks* that give tips to newcomers, help with making contacts, but also quickly communicate professional trends is almost a must for online journalists. Here we have also listed useful databases and contact exchanges.
2. *Journals* can also be helpful, especially if they are also available online.
3. *Prizes and scholarships* are not only interesting for beginners, but also for professionals.

Journalists' unions and networks have good contact offers, especially for freelancers. The Bavarian Journalists' Association has set up a regulars' table for online journalists in Munich. There are similar events in other cities – it is best to ask directly. Contact the association: *German Journalists' Association* (http://www.djv.de) and via the regional associations.

"Mediafon" is the name of the counselling service for freelance journalists offered by the *dju in the ver.di trade union* (http://www.mediafon.net).

Social networks such as *Facebook* or *Xing* offer topic-oriented groups for online journalism, online PR and cross-media work. Registered users can search the profiles of other community members by keywords. Online networks are a good way for online journalists to get to know colleagues and to exchange ideas with them, to make new contacts and to maintain existing ones.

There are excellent seminar exchanges online for online journalists. The database *Course* of the *Federal Employment Office* is an extensive collection of training and further education opportunities: from 1-day or weekend seminars to courses lasting several years. By entering keywords, offers from the online journalistic field can be researched. The database can be accessed via http://www.arbeitsagentur.de.

The *Media Study Guide* at http://www.medien-studienfuehrer.de provides information on more than 300 media *study* courses. The Mediencampus Bayern (http://www.mediencampusbayern.de) also provides information on current courses in its media wiki (http://www.medienwiki.org).

There are many jobs offered on the internet, usually also free *internships.* You can find offers at trade journals or publishers, but also at the employment agency:
http://www.arbeitsagentur.de
http://www.newsroom.de
http://www.kress.de
http://www.wuv.de
http://www.horizontjobs.de
http://www.dwdl.de

The job meta-search engine of the *Zeit* can be reached via http://jobs.zeit.de/.

Magazines and newsletters: The following list gives a selection of the regular publications relevant to online journalists; however, the proportion for the topic of online journalism varies greatly.

The Annenberg School of Journalism publishes the excellent *Online Journalism Review* newsletter: http://www.ojr.org. The newsletter is free of charge; interested parties can subscribe online.

The German-language site http://www.onlinejournalismus.de provides information about trends in the profession. It was awarded the Grimme Online Award. One can subscribe to the RSS feeds and follow on social media.

https://netzpolitik.org, which can also be subscribed to as a feed or via social media, provides information about the latest articles on journalism, new media and politics.

The highest-circulation association-oriented trade journal is the monthly *Journalist* of the German Journalists' Association. Excerpts can be read at http://www.journalist-magazin.de.

The magazine *M – Menschen machen Medien* contains contributions from the *German Journalists' Union (dju)* in Verdi, appears several times a year and is available online in its entirety (http://mmm.verdi.de).

Medium Magazin (http://www.mediummagazin.de) is a trade journal independent of any association. It informs about trends in the journalistic trade in general, about training and jobs.

Studies on the use of electronic media are contained in the magazine *Media-Perspektiven*, published on behalf of the Working Group of the ARD Advertising Companies (http://www.media-perspektiven.de).

15 subjectively selected tips,
who to follow on Twitter:

* ARDZDF Media Academy @ARDZDF_Akademie
* Björn Staschen @BjoernSta
* Data journalist @datajournalist
* DLFMedia @DLFmedien
* epd media @epdmedia
* JournalistPrizes @jourprizes
* #medianoise @medianoise
* MEDIA360G @MEDIA360G
* Nea Matzen @Nea_Matzen
* New German Media Makers @NDMedienmacher
* Matthias Spielkamp @spielkamp
* t3n Magazine @t3n
* What with media @whatwithmedia
* ZAPP Media Magazine @ZappMM
* and if you are interested Gabriele Hooffacker @ghooffacker.

Through competitions and prizes, you can learn a lot, but also gain contacts, a lot of honor and sometimes some money.

The Adolf Grimme Institute awards the *Grimme Prize* annually for outstanding achievements in professional journalism. Since 2001, a separate online award has been presented: Grimme Online Award (http://www.grimme-institut.de).

The *Axel Springer Prize for Young Journalists* is also awarded in the Internet category (http://www.axel-springer-akademie.de/axel-springer-preis.html).

Of interest to professionals and citizen journalists alike is the *Alternative Media Prize*, which the Nuremberg Media Academy awards annually together with the *Journalism Academy Foundation* (http://www.alternativer-medienpreis.de).

Because all these offers with their web addresses are subject to frequent changes, we recommend the updated version on http://www.onlinejournalismus.org.

Further Reading

1. La Roches Einführung in den praktischen Journalismus. Mit genauer Beschreibung aller Ausbildungswege, Deutschland, Österreich, Übersicht über Wege in den Journalismus auf: http://www.praktischer-journalismus.de

Glossary[1]

360-degree images This requires a 360-degree camera system. Mostly, the so-called stitching is used, the compilation of many individual images.

5G Standard for mobile internet and mobile telephony that builds on the existing mobile communications standard "Long Term Evolution" → LTE. It is intended to enable data rates of up to 10 Gbit/s and much higher data throughput. Other features include real-time transmission and latency times of a few milliseconds to less than one millisecond.

Access authorization → Account.

Accessibility The principle that as few access barriers as possible should be created when designing websites. Such obstacles can lie in the physical impairment of a user as well as in the hardware or software used.

Account User account, whether paid or not. Consists of the user's name and a password.

Affiliation Revenue-oriented online sales concept in the context of → e-commerce, in which commission is paid for the products sold.

Aggregator Database-based online service that collects → content and recompiles it according to selected criteria. A well-known news aggregator is Google News.

Ajax *Asynchronous JavaScript and XML* is a mixture of different web techniques and became popular in connection with Web 2.0. Through → asynchronous data

---

[1] In this chapter I explain online-typical technical terms and abbreviations. If you want to know where certain terms appear in the book, use the search function.

© Springer Fachmedien Wiesbaden GmbH, part of Springer Nature 2022
G. Hooffacker, *Online journalism*,
https://doi.org/10.1007/978-3-658-35731-3

transfer between browser and server, it becomes possible to exchange individual components of a web page without reloading the entire page.

Algorithm Rule-based action procedure for computing processes or solving problems. In both search engine optimization and social media, algorithms determine what content we get to see.

AMA "Ask me anything," format on Reddit. In an AMA post, a user answers all questions posed by the Reddit community.

Analytics Analysis of user behavior data. One well-known method of data collection is the use of a tracking tag (tracking marker) on a website. The tool starts a "session" as soon as a user visits the website, and then stores all the data about which pages the user was on, how long he stayed there, and how he interacted with the page elements.

Anchor Jump target, which is usually within the same document as the jump label. The user reaches a destination further down, outside the field of view, but within the same document, via → hyperlink.

Android Operating system for mobile devices provided free of charge by Google, currently the most common mobile operating system on smartphones. Manufacturers such as Samsung, HTC, Huawei or LG use Android.

API *Application Programming* Interface.

ASCII *American Standard Code for Information Interchange,* includes the Latin alphabet in upper and lower case, the ten Arabic numerals and some punctuation and control characters. The character set largely corresponds to that of a keyboard or typewriter for the English language.

Asset The individual components of a website that make up the → content: text, image, sound or video files.

Asset Management Component of the → CMS that manages the → assets and organizes the separation of content and layout.

Asynchronous time-shifted, asynchronous online forms of presentation contrast with → synchronous or "live" forms.

Atom usually the *Atom Syndication Format for* the platform-independent exchange of information, see also → RSS.

Attachment Attachment or attachment to the e-mail.

Audio From lat. audire = to hear. Component of words having to do with hearing or with sound. Examples: Real Audio, MP3, MIDI, WAV, AU.

Authoring system Software for designing multimedia products for CD-ROM and Internet.

Avatar three-dimensional online representation of people.

B2B (Business to Business) The target group for this → e-business strategy is business customers. Characteristics are few high-value transactions, functional design and often password-protected access.

B2C (Business to Consumer) Private customers are the target group here, characteristics: many transactions with low value, elaborate design, high promotion effort.

Backlink Link that leads from other websites to your own website. For Google, the number of backlinks is important for the ranking of the corresponding website.

Bandwidth Speed at which data can be transported over an online connection.

Banner Advertising spaces on the web that refer to the online offer of the advertiser via hyperlink. They consist of (1) the graphic, (2) the so-called alternative text to the graphic, (3) the link.

Big Data Very large amounts of unstructured data, mostly from users. The goal is to sort, analyze and process this data.

Bit From binary *digit* = binary number. Designation for a binary digit (usually "0" and "1"), the smallest unit of measurement for data.

Blog → Weblog.

Bookmark → Bookmark.

Bookmark stores web addresses like in an address book → social bookmarking.

Bot of robots, program-controlled interaction with the user. Bots are used in relationship management for frequently occurring routine questions from users, see also → Avatar.

Branding Conception and development of a brand product, for example an online offer.

Browser Software required to view → web pages. Examples: Firefox, Internet Explorer.

Buffer → Buffer.

Buffer Data buffer for → streams, which is created for a few seconds before the streaming file is played in order to prevent the display from tearing off in the event of poor connections.

Button *Button*, graphical button that is usually accompanied by a link.

Cache A temporary storage facility for data in order to increase the speed of operation.

Cascading style sheets Style sheets for font size, color and font type of a → web page. Frames or backgrounds can also be set up via stylesheet.

CGI Common Gateway Interface, standardized programming interface for data exchange between browser and programs on the web server.

Channel Channel, usually topic-oriented section of an online service, e.g. in chat.

Chat Online conference where you talk live in writing or verbally with other participants.

Clickbait → teaser with a misleading or sensational headline that entices users to click on the whole story. This is intended to increase the number of page views and thus advertising revenue.

Client retrieves services from another program, usually the server.

Client Side Image Maps graphics broken down into subareas that lead to various documents. They are evaluated by the browser.

CMS Content management system, also: editorial system, program for the planned creation, processing, organization and archiving of data.

Collaborative Multi-author projects are created through collaborative writing. Example: → Wikis like Wikipedia.

Common Gateway Interface → CGI.

Community Community, also: Virtual Community (VC), communication-oriented online service for users with similar interests.

Content Editorial content of a website, which can consist not only of text but also of images, audio and video elements and database content → Assets.

Content Authoring Program that automatically controls the display of → content. As a rule, → script languages are used for this purpose.

Content management covers all online journalistic tasks related to multimedia information in digital form, from procurement and editing to design and publication. The aim is to automate editorial processes as far as possible. Editorial systems or → CMS are used for this purpose.

Content Management System → CMS.

Content provider Editorial Content Merchants → Content Syndication.

Content repository Digital storage system for → assets and the associated → meta information, can be organized as a file system, a database or a mixture of both.

Content syndication similarly, content sharing: exchange of or trade in editorial content for online media.

Content-Life-Cycle describes the stages through which an → asset passes from the idea to archiving.

Cookies File entries that are used by the online provider to recognise the user. The cookie is stored in an area on the hard disk reserved for cookies by the → browser.

Copyright regulates the rights of authors.

Credits → Lead.

Crossmedia Across the media: → offer content not only for one medium, but for several media → content management.

CSS → Cascading Stylesheets.

Data mining Targeted evaluation of user profiles (profiling) according to interests, preferences, online behaviour, to be viewed critically from a data protection perspective.

Data protection Protection of the privacy of users of online services. Regulated by law in the Federal Republic of Germany, see chapter "Law".

Database colloquially refers to both the database server software and the data managed by it. Digital archives of all kinds – from photo to newspaper to film and music archives – are based on databases. See also content management.

Day Commands in → HTML are called "tags" and are enclosed in angle brackets.

Deep link complete path to the individual page in the → link.

Denic (German Network Information Center) a cooperative that allocates and manages → domains.

DHTML → Dynamic HTML.

DNS → Domain Name Service.

Document Management Program that manages and makes accessible unstructured information (full-text documents) in a database → content management.

Domain address globally unique address of a website, for example "http://www.journalistenakademie.de". The domain address puts the technical → IP address behind it into a format that people can remember.

Domain Name Service (DNS): Information service for Internet computers, which refers from the easy-to-remember plain text names such as "http://www.bundesregierung.de" to the → *IP address* behind it. Servers and clients rely on its information for data communication.

Dossier → Network dossier.

DRM Digital Rights Management, collective term for technical procedures for the protection of copyrights.

DTD Document type definition, describes documents of a certain type. The structure of the document is defined in a DTD.

Dynamic pages → Web pages that automatically change their content. Example: the price development of the Microsoft share over the course of the last week.

E-Business Online mapping of all commercial transactions.

E-commerce Online mapping of the commercial processes involved in selling products and services.

E-Learning Online or offline form of learning that is controlled by the learner. Other terms for online learning are also "telelearning" or "web-based training" (WBT).

Edit individual change to an online document. For conflicts in → collaborative writing occasionally lead to the dreaded *edit war.*

Editorial system Software for → content management and online publishing that coordinates all editorial processes.

Edutainment Artificial word made up of education and entertainment, combining education and entertainment, particularly important online in → e-learning.

Extranet Closed user group; extends the circle of authorised → intranet users to include external employees or sales partners. Characterized by password-protected access to a defined area.

FAQ Frequently Asked Questions, collection of frequently asked questions and the corresponding answers from all areas. There are FAQs on computer topics as well as on authors or musicians.

Feed Subscribable news in short form or → teaser. Feeds are offered on news sites, weblogs and podcasts to inform about contributions on this website. On their own desktop, visitors can see whether there are any articles of interest to them → Atom, RSS.

Feedreader (also known as "feed reader" or "input reader"), also known as → **aggregator,** program for reading in and processing feeds.

File Transfer Protocol (FTP): an Internet standard, protocol and application to perform simple and fast file transfer between two computer systems.

Firewall Firewall, electronic protective wall to prevent the spying out of data on one's own → server, cf. → data protection.

Flame verbal attack on another net participant. The *Flame Wars are* feared, insult wars that can paralyze entire discussion forums.

Flash Tool of the company Macromedia, with which multimedia web applications (Flash movies, background music) can be developed.

Flat rate Fixed price with no time or usage based charges.

Folksonomy Made up of "folks" and "taxonomy", collaborative rating of products as well as links. Products as well as links.

Followers User who has subscribed to the → feed of another user, for example on → Twitter.

Follow-up One or more replies to a message.

Form → Form of presentation.

Formats (1) (journalistic) In radio and television journalism, the formal and content-related framework of a programme. Online journalism formats make use of the → interactive and → participative possibilities online. (2) (techn.): Depending on the application program, files are available in defined formats, for example in → HTML format on the → web.

Forms of presentation Journalistic text types, which in traditional journalism are divided into informative and commentary forms. Online, a distinction is made between → interactive and → participative forms, but also between → synchronous or "live" forms and → asynchronous forms.

Forum Forums or groups go back to the classic Internet service "News", which was invented at universities: Requests and offers are published like on a bulletin board.

Frame Frame, design technique that divides the browser window into several independent areas.

Frameset defines the division of the browser window into → frames.

FTP → File Transfer Protocol.

Geo-tagging also known as **georeferencing,** assigns spatial information, the georeference, to a data set. Example: Local news can be assigned to points on a map.

GIF *Graphics Interchange Format,* a graphics standard coined by Compuserve that compresses images to a minimum of space without loss of information.

GPL General Public License, license for the general public, distribution concept for software or content. In this case, the distributor undertakes to charge only distribution or support costs and to make the source code available to the user.

GPRS Standard for data transmission, which allows up to 53.6 kBit/s. With this, reasonable internet use is hardly possible any more.

Guestbooks/Diaries Web presentation form that publishes user contributions, often in real time, sometimes also moderated. Special form: →Weblogs, blogs for short, which also offer discussion forums.

GUI Graphical User Interface, graphical interface through which the user accesses a program.

Hashtag Keyword in → Twitter. Origin: *hash* = English for the hash sign #. Example: "#hashtag". Hashtags are inserted directly into the actual message.

Hit Access to the individual file. An HTML page can consist of one or many files – depending on how many graphic or other media elements are used, cf. → PageImpression (PI).

Home page → Homepage.

Homepage Start or entry page of a → website.

Host A single computer in a network that acts as a "host computer", providing data or computing time to others.

HSDPA High Speed Downlink Packet Access, also called **3G +.** This enables data transmission of up to 13.96 MBit/s.

HTML The Web uses the Hypertext Markup Language (HTML) language to describe the layout of documents.

HTTP The Hypertext Transfer Protocol (HTTP) is used on the → Web to access documents at destinations anywhere on the network.

Hyperlink Linking of the individual parts of a hypertext, cf. → Link.

Hypermedia Linking of various media elements within the framework of a → hypertext system.

Hypertext system According to this system, texts that are distributed across the entire network can be linked by means of keywords (→ link). Each keyword refers to a different part of the text or text.

Imprint information on the publisher, author, editor or editorial staff required for publications in order to identify those responsible for the content under press law.

Infotainment An artificial word made up of information and entertainment, combining entertaining and informative elements in one article.

Instant Messaging (IM) Personal, synchronous, software-supported communication between two or more people online.

Interactive Interactive is the term used for program interfaces with which the user can communicate, examples: a shopping cart that the user compiles according to his or her individual needs, or a hypertext structure through which the user clicks by selecting with the mouse.

Internet The entirety of online interaction and communication options available to all users. The technical basis is the Internet Protocol (R IP, → TCP/IP) transmission standard. The possibilities offered by the internet include not only → web and → e-mail, but also → news, → ftp, → chat and much more. Cf. also → Intranet.

Interstate Broadcasting Treaty (RStV): State treaty between all German federal states that created uniform federal regulations for broadcasting law. Will be replaced by the State Media Treaty in 2020.

Intranet describes a closed network of a precisely defined number of users: the employees of one's own company. They have their own access authorisations (R accounts) and have read and write rights graded according to function. See also → Extranet.

iOS Operating system developed by Apple and used on all iPhones and iPads.

IP stands for Internet Protocol, the transmission standard on which the → Internet is based. The Internet Protocol can transport a data packet along various paths via several different computer platforms until it reaches its destination.

IP address Unique 4-byte address available to every computer on the Internet, a prerequisite for data exchange via the Internet. Example: 220.120.50.1 For humans, the → domain address is sufficient.

IPTC The International Press Telecommunications Council (IPTC) sets worldwide standards in the field of platform-independent information capture and processing. To define the structure and content of multimedia data, the IPTC has created the → Newsml standards, and for text documents → NITF.

IRC Internet Relay Chat, a service on the Internet that enables simultaneous communication with any number of participants. An IRC user connects to one of the numerous constantly active channels and can then participate 'live' in the discussion currently taking place there, cf. → Chat.

Java Object-oriented, platform-independent programming language, designed for use in networks with different computer systems.

Javascript Programming language for simple control tasks in the World Wide Web, such as navigation between several pages or simple input checks.

JPEG (JPG) Graphic format defined by the *Joint Photographic Experts Group*. The file size is compressed.

Knowledge Management *Knowledge management,* all operational activities and management tasks aimed at the best possible handling of knowledge. Technically, a → CMS is used for this purpose.

Labeling the art of labelling → navigation elements in a meaningful way.

Landing page a specially created website to which the click on an entry in a search engine leads. The landing page is optimized for the target group.

Launch Repositioning of an (online) product on the market, cf. → Relaunch.

Lead The lead of the article, usually printed in bold type.

Liability (for online offers) the imputability or obligation to pay damages.

License → Copyright.

Linear/non-linear Online offers do not consist of a continuous (linear) text, but of several files that are linked to each other, cf. →Link. The order in which the user clicks on them is not fixed.

Link Connection, also hyperlink. In terms of server technology, a distinction is made between on-page links that lead to a jump target within the present document (→anchor), on-site links that remain within the online offering but refer to a new document, and external links that lead to another server.

Link consistency If all links of a → website point correctly to their target, if there are no links that lead nowhere and no orphaned pages to which no link points, this is called link consistency.

Linux Operating system that is subject to the → GPL.

Live → synchronous.

Live content Content that is produced and encoded at the same time as it is broadcast to the web to create a live stream.

Live streaming the transmission of streaming content to the user simultaneously with its creation.

LTE Mobile communications standard, which is also referred to as 4th generation – hence **4G**. With LTE, transmission speeds of up to 300 MBit/s are possible.

Mailing list Distribution service for e-mails.

Markup language Assigns properties or attributes ("bold", "heading") to text elements. Example: → HTML.

Mashup Web content (text, data, images, sounds or videos) is combined with other applications, for example linked to geographical data. Mashups use → APIs for this purpose.

Mem Mostly visually implemented theme that is transferred to further persons or contexts. The term goes back to Richard Dawkins. According to him, memes are ideas that are copied and combined from one person to another, analogous to genes that are passed on from one generation to the next.

Message informative → form of presentation. Preparing a message for the screen means above all: finding out what is essential, what is current, what is special and distributing it over teasers and text.

Meta language from Greek *meta* = afterwards, after, → markup language for defining other languages.

Meta tags HTML commands that store additional information in the head of an HTML document, i.e. invisible to the user.

Metadata from Greek *meta* = after; data containing information about other data, for example, information about the properties of an object, such as the author's name or the date of creation.

Me-too "find' ich auch": unsolicited response in → mailing lists.

MMS Multimedia Message Service, mobile phone service which, in addition to e-mail, also allows the sending of sound, specialist graphics, videos and other files.

Motion tracking Motion capture, tracking method used to capture user movements. It converts the movement into a computer-readable format, analyzes it and records it. Common methods are head tracking or eye tracking. The tracking data can be used to transfer motion sequences into virtual reality productions, which can be used to interact with users in gaming, for example.

MPEG Compression method for moving pictures, acronym of the *Moving Picture Experts Group.*

Multimedia A dazzling term that also encompasses telecommunications and online services. At least three communication channels – image, sound, text – combine to form "multimedia".

Namespace Namespaces are technically used to prevent conflicts in naming. Example: → DNS.

Navigation Movement of the user within a → site. Making navigation between channels and within the site as easy and pleasant as possible for the user (R Convenience, → Usability) should be the common goal of both online journalists and screen designers.

Navigation bar A navigation bar is similar to a table of contents and consists of the – preferably apt or "speaking" – texts or symbols for the individual sections of the website, which are backed up with links.

Navigation point Text or picture element that creates the link to the subsequent document in the background.

Net Report Online format, provides the user with an overview of a current topic in the main text, for example "Right-wing extremism on the Internet". Hot words in the text link to the addressed, mostly external sources; below the text or in a separate column, the links are listed again systematically and often also commented on.

Network dossier Online format consisting of several own contributions to a topic; it usually contains internal as well as external links.

News aggregator → Aggregator.

News Feed → Feed.

News ML International → IPTC standard for managing digital data (text, image, audio, video).

News Internet form in which news from any user is distributed around the world and made available to all other users. The news is divided into more than a thousand topic groups with several hundred thousand news items per day.

Newsdesk Workplace in the *newsroom* where current reports are received. Derived from this, it means a form of organization in editorial departments in which department heads from different departments sit at a common table and decide on the output route. The prerequisite for setting up newsdesks is an editorial system that allows access to all multimedia elements at all times.

Newsgroups also → forums where users leave → news.

Newsletter Print: a compact information carrier of a few pages. Online: subscribed information service that is automatically delivered to the user's e-mail box on a regular basis.

Newsreader Utility for reading and writing in → newsgroups.

Newsroom → Newsdesk.

NITF News Industry Text Format; international → IPTC standard for text documents.

Node or (tree) knot an element, an attribute, a comment or a text within a → markup language. From each node, sub-elements can in turn branch off, which in turn can act as nodes, creating a document tree.

Non-linear → linear.

Odds means for → e-mail and → news: quoting from the original message to which you are replying.

On-Demand Content Content that is not produced and made available for → live streaming but for permanent retrieval.

Online Data is transferred or processed when there is a connection to another computer or data network. Contrast: *offline.*

Online first principle that articles are already available online before the subsequent print edition. Publishing news on the web thus takes precedence over publication in the print medium.

Page → page.

Page *Page*, continuous online document with → links, not to be confused with the content of a → screen page.

Page description language describes how a page should later look in a special output program.

Page impression (PI), refers to the number of times users view an HTML page. A PI usually comprises several → hits. For offers with frames, only the first call of a frame set counts as PI. More meaningful: → Visit.

Page rank algorithm Procedure for evaluating linked documents used by Google. In this process, each element is assigned a weight, the page rank, based on its linking structure. The algorithm was developed by Larry Page (hence the name PageRank) and Sergei Brin at Stanford University.

Parser Computer program responsible for breaking down and converting any input into a format that can be used for further processing.

Participatory Participative forms are forms of online exchange in which at least two people communicate with each other, from e-mail to discussion forum to chat, cf. → interactive.

Partner programs → Affiliation.

PDF The *Portable Document Format* (PDF) is a page description language and was designed as an exchange format for finished documents. With the help of PDF, documents can be printed, sent and archived true to the original. It is a document-final format that allows few changes to the document.

Peer-to-peer equal communication, counterpart: server-client.

PERL *Practical Extension and Report Language*, a freely available programming language used especially for writing CGI scripts on Internet servers.

Permalink URL address of a specific content. You can find the permalink of a content by clicking its timestamp.

PHP *PHP Hypertext Preprocessor,* server-side scripting language, currently: PHP4.

PI → Page Impression.

Pingback allows to request a notification as soon as someone links the own documents or web pages.→ Trackback.

Pixel Smallest unit of a digital overview graphic, artificial word from the abbreviation of the English words picture and element.

Plug-In Auxiliary program for the → browser that is installed on the user's computer. Example: "Acrobat Reader" from Adobe for PDF files.

Podcast Offering media files (audio or video) that can be subscribed to via → feed. The word is composed of the words *iPod* (MP3 player from Apple) and *broadcasting.*

Portal Entry page to the web that promises information seekers quick orientation in the online world.

Post, posting stands for sending a digital message.

Press code journalistic-ethical basic rules in the form of a voluntary commitment, which the German Press Council defines and updates.

Profiling Data collection about user habits → data mining.

Protocol self-imposed, binding rules or standards for the communication of computers or networks with each other.

Provider Company that brokers access to all Internet services: Internet Service Provider (ISP). Web space providers or e-mail providers, for example, specialize in individual services. In contrast, content providers take care of the editorial content.

Proxy server Temporary storage for frequently used information from the Internet; can be located at the provider's, but also in the company, in order to keep the network load and access times low.

Pull The term "pull" stands for individualized forms of communication: The user decides for himself which and how much information he wants to receive.

Push Push" stands for the active transmission of documents from the server to the client. With push technology, servers automatically transmit new news and interesting content – without any action on the part of the reader. The reader simply subscribes to a few channels (R Channels) and automatically receives the latest information during each web visit.

Quote "Quotation". If you refer to a text passage of the original mail when replying to a message, you use a quotation mark: The text parts of the mail are specially marked in the first line, for example with ">".

Raffles → Games.

Realtime in real time, live, also → synchronous, cf. → streaming media.

Referrer electronic recording of which website the user comes from.

Relaunch Complete revision including new design (redesign) of a website. Counterpart: → Launch.

Report → Network Report.

RSS Really Simple Syndication, → XML-based format for exchanging content.

RSS feed News output in RSS format; informs the user in the form of a summary about news on a website.

Screen English screen page.

Screen Design Designing for the screen as opposed to the layout of a newspaper or magazine.

Screen page → Screen.

Script language Programming languages such as → CGI, → Perl, → PHP.

Scroll Scroll, list; continue to the next screen section, "scroll".

Search Engine Online service for keyword-based retrieval of online information. A so-called agent (also: spider, robot) searches everything on the web that it can find and evaluates it according to keywords (*meta tags*) or full text. The terms are recorded and cross-referenced to the page on which they can be found. The entire system consisting of search program, address base, evaluation program and database is called a "search engine".

Search engine optimization (*Search Engine Optimization*, SEO for short): Improving the ranking of websites in search engines. This includes adherence to standards, finding suitable search terms, search term density, use of search terms in page titles (title tag), headings, text links and within the → URL.

Semantic Web (English *Semantic Web*), extension of the World Wide Web with the aim of making the meaning of information usable for computers.

Sentiment analysis Digital evaluation of linguistically expressed emotions based on data collected online. With the help of linguistic data processing or other computer analysis methods, the aim is to find out what attitude is hidden behind a post on social media.

SEO → Search Engine Optimization.

Server *Server;* computer that provides storage and processing tasks for other network participants *(clients).*

SGML From *Standard Generalized Markup Language* = standardized generalized markup language. SGML is a meta language that can be used to define different markup languages for documents.

Signature *Signature,* identification lines of an Internet subscriber. E-mail programs automatically add the signature to the message content. In accordance with → TMG, it should contain the complete contact details.

Site The entire online offering, consisting of a → homepage and any number of other → pages.

Skype Software for making free calls via the Internet *(Voice over IP)* and chargeable calls to landlines and mobile phones *(SkypeOut)* with → instant messaging function, file transfer and video telephony.

Slideshow Multimedia presentation form in online journalism, usually an animated photo series accompanied by a parallel soundtrack.

SMS Short Message Service, short message service on mobile phones that enables the bidirectional transmission of short messages (up to 160 characters).

Social bookmarking Collaborative and public provision and addition of bookmarks (→ bookmark) lists.

Social media → Social networks on the Internet that serve to exchange → content. See also → User Generated Content.

Social media optimization (SMO) Optimization of web pages so that they are better received by social media services and other websites. Among other things, RSS feeds or links to social bookmarking services serve this purpose.

Social network Online service that provides a network community with various communication options, including collaborative working and rating. See also → Community.

Source text describes the structure of a web page.

Spam "Spiced Pork And Ham" or "Specially Prepared Assorted Meat", originally unpopular tinned meat made famous by a Monty Python sketch. On the Internet: Advertising via mass-mailed posts.

State Media Treaty A set of rules on the regulation of media offerings and providers, which will come into force in the course of 2020.

Storyboard Overview plan containing all → pages and, in some cases, also the → assets of an online offering, including links.

Stream individual transmission to the user.

Streaming Technology with which video and audio data are processed in such a way that → synchronous real-time audio and video reception (R real-time) from the Internet is made possible. The data is played back while it is being downloaded and does not have to be saved in its entirety first.

Stylebook/Styleguide In-house "etiquette" for consistent online navigation and design.

Stylesheet defines several properties of text elements such as font type, size or color, cf. Cascading Stylesheets.

Synchronous Online form of presentation that is → broadcast live. Chat and dynamic pages belong to the "live" forms, contr: → asynchronous.

Tag cloud Keyword cloud, is created from keywords and used to structure blog content.

Teaser *To tease, tease*, tease: In online journalism, short texts, often with a picture, that are intended to tease the user into clicking further.

Telemedia Act regulates the legal framework in Germany for so-called telemedia, i.e. almost all electronic information and communication services.

Teletext → Teletext.

Teletext Service of the television broadcasters. Originally in the so-called blanking interval, today as a digital stream, standing "panels" are broadcast with subtitles, program notes, news and weather reports.

Template Website Creation Template.

Thread *Thread*: The original message and all subsequent replies in a discussion forum together make up a thread.

Throwback Thursday (#tbt) Social media tradition of posting a weekly post with historical content. Throwback Thursday was particularly popular on Instagram.

Time-to-Web Time required from conception to publication on the → web. It determines the update frequency of the → website.

TMG → Telemedia Act.

Trackback Function that allows weblogs to exchange information about backlinks with each other in the form of reactions or comments through an automatic notification service.

Traffic Utilization of a server by active users.

Troll *trolling* = fishing with a trolling line; provocateur who distracts from the actual topic of discussion in discussion forums. Therapy: *"Don't feed the troll"*.

Tunnel structure Hypertext sequence that takes away the user's autonomy of action and, under certain circumstances, time: He must submit to a predetermined sequence of pages.

Twitter → Social network with diary-like short entries on the Internet (microblog). Registered users can enter text messages with a maximum of 140 characters and send them to other users. Posts on Twitter are known as *"tweets"*. → followers.

UGC → User Generated Content.

UMTS Universal Mobile Telecommunications System(s). Mobile communications standard that offers higher à bandwidths: Internet access with a data transmission speed of up to two megabits per second (mbps) is possible from a UMTS mobile phone.

URL Uniform Resource Locator, the location or address of a document on the Internet. The first digits indicate which transmission protocol and which service are involved. Example: "http:" for → Web.

Usability "Usability" of a website. The term was created by Jakob Nielsen.

Usenet Selection of certain globally distributed → newsgroups.

User Participant, user or operator.
User-generated content user-created content, especially in → social networks.
Vector graphic Computer image composed of lines, circles and polygons.
Video From Latin videre = to see, used in speech as a component of words having to do with moving pictures, e.g. video cassette, video camera.
Video formats Recording method for electronic recordings of moving images. File-based formats basically encode the video information digitally, while video tape formats store information in analog or digital form. Occasionally, television formats (HDTV, NTSC, PAL, SECAM, DVB, ATSC, ISDB) are also referred to as video formats.
Virtual community → Community.
Virtual community User communities with common interests, cf. → Community.
Virtual reality Virtual reality (VR) refers to the representation and perception of a computer-generated reality. VR glasses of various systems, motion tracking, eye tracking, controllers and other aids allow the user to immerse himself in the virtual world. If the thought of the real world is pushed further and further into the background, the effect is called *immersion*. Virtual reality is not only used for games and entertainment, but also offers media possibilities to explain their topics interactively, for example in an explainer video.
Viruses, computer virus Self-replicating program that may destroy data and programs. Virus programs can only sit in executable programs.
Visit The longer a user spends on a website, the more pages he views and the longer he stays. Such a coherent usage process or visit is referred to as a visit. According to IVW, it defines the advertising medium contact. See also → Hit, → Page Impression.
Vlog V(ideo-B)log, is a made-up word from → video and → blog, website that periodically contains new entries (majority or exclusively) as video. Form of activity: vlogging.
Vodcast Video Podcast, → Podcast.
Voice over IP telephony (short for *Internet Protocol Telephony*), also **Internet telephony, is telephoning** via the Internet. See also → Skype.
WCMS → Content Management System.
Web 2.0 Buzzword used to describe a range of interactive and collaborative elements of the Internet.
Web cam 1. Camera for livestream, 2. → synchronous visual format with still or moving image, proves the authenticity of what is shown.
Webcam 1. Special camera, 2. synchronous visual format with still or moving image, proves the authenticity of what is shown.

Weblog Blogs for short, a further development of → guestbook/diary and → forum under a web interface. This format combines the possibility of communication provided by a forum with hypertext.

Website → page.

Website → Site.

Wording (Marketing) word choice when copywriting a web page.

Workflow Workflow in an online editorial department, largely determined by the → CMS.

Workflow management maps, controls and manages the editorial workflows in the → CMS.

World Wide Web (WWW), Internet service whose → pages are linked via → links to → hypertext. Concept: Tim Berners-Lee (1991). Since the web combines text, image, audio and video files under its graphical interface to form → hypermedia, it has become the most popular service on the internet alongside e-mail.

XHTML from Extensible Hypertext Markup Language = extensible HTML, the XML variant of HTML. All elements of HTML 4.0/4.01 are defined in such a way that they correspond to the specifications and requirements of XML. XHTML is therefore an application of XML.

Xlink Defines the inclusion of links in XML documents.

XML *Extensible Markup Language*, not a page description language like HTML, but a tool for designing your own language elements and languages, each adapted to a specific purpose.

XSL *Extensible Stylesheet Language,* similar to CSS, a kind of format template for the layout of a web page and describes the representation and handling of XML data with the help of XSL stylesheets.

Further Links

1. https://journalistikon.de
2. http://en.wikipedia.org

© Springer Fachmedien Wiesbaden GmbH, part of Springer Nature 2022
G. Hooffacker, *Online journalism*,
https://doi.org/10.1007/978-3-658-35731-3

Printed in the United States
by Baker & Taylor Publisher Services